1987 BIENNIAL EXHIBITION

1987

BIENNIAL

EXHIBITION

RICHARD ARMSTRONG

JOHN G. HANHARDT

RICHARD MARSHALL

LISA PHILLIPS

WHITNEY MUSEUM OF AMERICAN ART, NEW YORK

in association with

W.W. NORTON & COMPANY, NEW YORK, LONDON

EXHIBITION SCHEDULE

Fourth floor, Lobby Gallery, and Lower Gallery
April 10–July 5

Second floor and Second-floor Film/Video Gallery
March 31–June 28

THIS EXHIBITION IS SPONSORED BY AMERICAN CAN COMPANY FOUNDATION,
JAY CHIAT FOUNDATION, AND THE NATIONAL ENDOWMENT FOR THE ARTS.

LIBRARY OF CONGRESS CATALOGING-IN PUBLICATION DATA

1987 Biennial exhibition, Whitney Museum of American Art, New York.

Bibliography: p.
1. Arts, American—Exhibitions. 2. Arts, Modern—
20th century—United States—Exhibitions. I. Armstrong,
Richard. II. Whitney Museum of American Art.
NX504.A1A17 1987   700'.973'07401471 87-2179
ISBN 0-87427-052-9
ISBN 0-393-30439-6 (trade paperback)

9
Foreword
TOM ARMSTRONG

11
Introduction
RICHARD ARMSTRONG, RICHARD MARSHALL, LISA PHILLIPS

17
Painting Sculpture Photography

147
Introduction to Film and Video
JOHN G. HANHARDT

153
Film and Video

183
Biographies

207
Works in the Exhibition

THE American Can Company Foundation and the Jay Chiat Foundation are pleased to join with the National Endowment for the Arts to sponsor the 1987 Biennial Exhibition at the Whitney Museum of American Art.

Since it began in 1932, the Biennial has become the most significant continuous series of survey exhibitions of contemporary American art. It presents works created during the previous two years by artists whom the curators believe are making statements of quality and particular importance. The Biennials often exhibit artists who are not well known and works which often provoke intense responses because they are not immediately or easily comprehensive. If the Biennial causes comment and controversy, that is as it should be. It is important for business to have concern for quality, personal accomplishments, and innovation, and to support similar considerations in the arts. For these reasons we are particularly pleased to support the 1987 Biennial Exhibition at the Whitney Museum of American Art.

WILLIAM S. WOODSIDE
Chairman, Executive Committee
American Can Company

JAY CHIAT
Chairman, Chief Executive Officer
Chiat/Day inc. Advertising

FOREWORD

THE GREATEST STRENGTH of the Whitney Museum of American Art throughout its history has been its primary commitment to present the work of living American artists. Among the most meaningful ways of expressing this commitment are the Biennial Exhibitions, a continuous series of survey exhibitions begun fifty-five years ago by Gertrude Vanderbilt Whitney, founder of the Whitney Museum. By encouraging members of the curatorial staff to exercise judgments about contemporary aesthetic achievements, the Biennial represents one of the most important components of the Museum's historical contribution to American culture. It is a collective statement intended to give the public an opportunity to see what we believe to be most compelling in the visual arts at a specific moment in our country's creative history.

The catalogue for this Biennial includes, in addition to John G. Hanhardt's survey of current activity in independent filmmaking and video art, an essay by the three other curators who organized the 1987 Biennial—Richard Armstrong, Richard Marshall, and Lisa Phillips. The essay explains how they decided on the scope and size of this Biennial and, more than in past years, places the artists selected in the context of contemporary aesthetic issues. The importance of this catalogue has been recognized by W.W. Norton & Co., who will distribute it commercially—a first for a Biennial catalogue.

To become a professional curator of contemporary art it is necessary not only to have knowledge and a knowing eye, but to be acquainted with many artists, to tolerate critical opinion, and to resist the innumerable pressures from all those who have a stake in the acceptance of an artist's work. As the staff makes decisions, I am constantly aware of how difficult it is to remain detached and to develop an unbiased point of view. I respect the curators who have organized this exhibition with individual conviction and dedication to their responsibilities on behalf of colleagues on the staff and the Trustees of the Museum. We are indebted to all of the lenders of works of art for their generosity and to the artists themselves whose talent and cooperation make possible everything we accomplish.

To pass judgment on contemporary art is risky business if you care about what other people think of your choices. At the heart of the Biennial—for the Museum and for the artists—is the belief in experimentation, in taking chances, and saying something in a new way, all of which generates dialogue and often controversy. The American Can Company has consistently helped the Museum in our most contemporary efforts, with grants to exhibitions such as "New Image Painting" (1978), the "1981 Biennial Exhibition," "Jonathan Borofsky" (1984), and "David Salle" (1987). Once again, through its enthusiastic support of the 1987 Biennial, the American Can Company Foundation has proven that a corporation can extend its adventurous spirit beyond business concerns to benefit the public.

This year, for the first time, we have also received significant support from an individual, Jay Chiat, through his foundation. We are extraordinarily grateful to him, because without his help, and that of American Can Company, the Biennial would not have been possible. We also extend our thanks to the National Endowment for the Arts, the third major contributor to the 1987 Biennial. This federal agency, more than any single source of funding, has consistently affirmed its belief in the importance of presenting contemporary art to the public through their support of exhibitions at the Whitney Museum of American Art.

We are grateful to our sponsors for another reason. Contemporary art activity now attracts an unprecedented number of wealthy individuals, many of whom begin to consider themselves as institutions as their judgments are reinforced by the actions of the market place. As this happens, their loyalty to established museums, and to the intellectual base they represent, is dissipated. It continues to be reassuring to us that there are individuals and corporations who put trust in the work of museum professionals dedicated to contemporary art and willing to take risks.

TOM ARMSTRONG
Director

INTRODUCTION

THE BIENNIAL EXHIBITION of the Whitney Museum of American Art is both an independent entity and part of a tradition begun more than half a century ago. Since 1932, each exhibition has become a chapter of a larger story—the curatorial perception of American art in evolution. As the only exhibition of its kind in New York and one of the oldest in the United States, the Biennial serves as a contemporary salon and as such has a forceful presence. Its regularity and close attention to the moment create wide expectations and generate considerable discussion.

There are certain elements in the exhibition's organizational process that produce a continuity with the past. First, the selection is the collaborative effort of a team of curators. At its inception, artists were chosen by the museum staff, though the works exhibited were left to the judgment of the artist. But by the 1940s, all exhibited work was selected by the Museum's curators. The founding philosophy of "no juries, no prizes" continues, as does the practice of purchasing works from the Biennial for the Permanent Collection. A second important constant is the focus on a specific time frame—the exhibitions began as biennials (1932–36), became annuals (1937–72), and reverted to biennials again in 1973. Thus the selections are intended to assess the present. A review of past exhibitions reveals that, historically, about half of the artists whose work is shown have been exhibited in earlier Biennials. The other half are newcomers, and for these first-time exhibitors, inclusion presents an opportunity to be considered in the company of established artists, itself a test of promise and strength. The Biennial can affect an artist's career by creating a context for positive critical reception. In other cases, however, artists who exhibit in a Biennial are never heard from again. The 1947 exhibition, for example, included not only Arshile Gorky, Jackson Pollock, and Ad Reinhardt, but also lesser-known, now almost forgotten artists, such as Hans Moller, Steve Raffo, and Georges Schreiber.

The Biennial has always been contentious. An event where aesthetic values, institutional power, financial interests, and artistic egos converge, it provokes outrage, comic one-liners, and most importantly an occasion to reflect on the state of contemporary art. Those searching for clear-cut definitions are inevitably disappointed, since the exhibition raises as many questions as it answers. Perhaps the most salient constants of the Biennials are the plaintive wails that greet it: "an exhibition predominantly given . . . to huge, formless, brash, blotchy, shapeless abstract-expressionist pictures so like each other that even a critic . . . is hard put to distinguish one from the other" (Emily Genauer, *New York Herald Tribune*, November 24, 1957); "If the current Whitney Biennial is not the worst major exhibition ever held in New York City, memory fails me" (Barbara Rose, *New York*, March 17, 1975); "It will hardly be a surprise to anyone, I suppose, to hear that the 1977 Whitney Biennial Exhibition ... is an unendurable bore" (Hilton Kramer, *New York Times*, February 27, 1977); "the worst in living memory..." (Robert Hughes, *Time*, June 17, 1985). Taking issue with the Biennial is part of the pleasure and part of the exhibition's history.

But other things about the Biennial do change. The criteria of selection are elastic enough to permit revision and responsiveness to current conditions. The strength of an artist's recent production is evaluated both in relation to that artist's entire body of work and in relation to the work of contemporaries. In addition, an artist's achievement is measured in the context of its current influence. Previous Biennial participation, as well as recent Whitney Museum exhibitions and soon-to-be presented ones are also evaluated by the curators to avoid overexposure and repetition.

For this Biennial, it was decided that the exhibition would benefit from a more rigorous selection process, with more works by fewer artists. A comprehensive cross section that reports on all the tendencies in American art is not possible today. Forty years ago, when the entire art community consisted of several hundred people, the notion of an all-inclusive presentation was feasible. Today, with more than 200,000 artists working in America (60,000 of them in New York), museums concerned with contemporary art have had to assume a more selective—more judgmental—role.

With an abundance of competent art and an audience with an insatiable appetite for the new, it is especially important that museums sort out what deserves distinction. In our selections we have been attentive to a range of visions and values and have sought to establish a sense of proportion and balance among them. As usual, some of the work on view is familiar because the artists have captured the attention of the media, while some is not well known, at least to general New York audiences. Nevertheless, the majority of these artists will be recognized by avid gallery visitors— another indication of how popular and well scrutinized the contemporary art scene has become.

The dominance of New York residents in this Biennial confirms the city's continuing strength as a cultural center. Often, however, the current residence of an artist is misleading. More than seventy percent of the New York-based artists in this Biennial were born and educated elsewhere (in twenty states and twelve foreign countries). Like other statistical aspects of Biennials, the percentage of non-New York-based artists has been fairly consistent, usually accounting for about one-third of the total.

After a decade of tacit disinterest in furthering the modernist project of abstraction, a number of younger artists have turned to nonrepresentational art as a fertile antidote to the expressionist figuration that has dominated most of the 1980s. Impatience with the melodramatic excesses of Neo-Expressionism has caused a highly touted shift toward a cool, hard-edged brand of abstraction variously dubbed "Smart Art," "Simulationism," and "Neo-Geo." But sloganeering has once again temporarily obfuscated the significant work in this genre and distorted the total range of types of abstraction.

Many artists are vitally concerned with developing an inclusive abstraction, one that tests the borders between naturalism and geometry. Abstraction today is not the closed, hermetic sort concerned principally with the internal language of art. Rather, it is expansive, and generated by a variety of natural and vernacular references, as seen in the obsessively autobiographical psychosexuality of Louise Bourgeois' sculpture; Lari Pittman's intricately painted gothic fantasies; Roberto Juarez's textured and interlocking planes of color and chronologically disjunctive images; and the gestural and physically improvisational modes of John Chamberlain, Alan Saret, and Stephen Mueller. A more iconic abstraction, loaded with real world quotations, is practiced by Peter Halley and R.M. Fischer. On a more ironic note are Philip Taaffe's collaged reconstructions of familiar art imagery.

There is a strong, romantic strain in much of this work. It is art full of poetic, mystical, and erotic force. A somber palette and the use of symbolic emblems to evoke an elegiac quality pervades works as otherwise disparate as Ross Bleckner's hazy nocturnes, Julian Schnabel's dark shrouds, and George Condo's melancholic visual riffs. These works suggest nineteenth-century Symbolism, where the experience of absence was made palpably present. They confront a growing sense of loss and a disequilibrium tinged with despondency.

Concurrent with the revived acceptance of abstract modes are the strong representational sensibilities common to the paintings of a number of artists included here. Robert Greene's arcadian reveries depict moody events in urbanized and romanticized landscapes. Jim Lute's horrific mental and urban landscapes, in contrast, reveal anatomical and natural elements that assume nightmarish meanings. David Bates' paintings use to advantage the physical relief of paint to underscore graphic American scene imagery. For Izhar Patkin the materiality of draped rubber becomes a support for his room-size narrative cycle of paintings. The theatricality of Patkin's presentation is underscored by its scale and physical drama. An abiding attention to craft and technique are integral to both Neil Jenney's and Robert Helm's exquisitely rendered trompe l'oeil scenes with frames specifically designed to enhance their illusionism. Similarly, Robert Lobe's enormous, handmade impressions of features in the landscape attest to the continuing inspiration of nature translated through physical processes.

In fact, making a physically compelling object is a common ambition of most of the artists in this Biennial. Material and process are symbiotically engaged in Donald Sultan's paintings of burning buildings, constructed by burning and cutting tar and linoleum. Terry Winters' analysis of paint pigments has often generated the molecular imagery that characterizes his work. Louise Fishman's dense structured impastos, Willem de Kooning's skein of lines, or Robert Ryman's combinations of gesture, paint, and support reaffirm that art is still celebrated as a sensual, physical activity. The role of the personalized gesture also continues to inform the planar accumulations of John Chamberlain's joined car parts, Alan Saret's aggregations of unbound wire, and Richard Tuttle's quixotic assemblages of urban detritus. Though all of this work demonstrates a physical confidence, it is conceptually more precise than much process and gesture-derived art of the 1960s, which required a rhetorical support and the physical euphoria of newly discovered materials to justify the aesthetic impulse.

Another striking feature of the work produced during the past two years is its search for rational order. Many younger artists acknowledge the value of Minimalist and Conceptualist ways of working, as is clear from the linguistic bent that coexists with the revival of geometric art. A number of works in the Biennial Exhibition are in fact generated by a desire to wed language and image: Judy Pfaff's aggressively three-dimensional sign-still lifes, Annette Lemieux's poignant use of found objects and phrases as mnemonic devices, Nancy Dwyer's amalgam of form and commercial cliché, and Barbara Kruger's graphic exhortations. David McDermott and Peter McGough's deliberately nostalgic content summons up a bygone era through words and a historical style that is infused with contemporary socio-sexual politics. In all this work, the fervor of Conceptualism is cross-fertilized with the irony of Pop. The results are disquieting, non-narrative, and exploit the fragmentation of contemporary life.

It is coincidental but significant that almost twenty years ago Conceptual art made its debut in Whitney Museum annuals: Edward Ruscha (1967), Richard Artschwager (1968), Joseph Kosuth (1969), Bruce Nauman (1969), and Neil Jenney (1969) were among its proponents then—and, to varying degrees, they remain so today. Kosuth's line-by-line obliteration of chosen texts and Ruscha's blank spaces emptied of words exemplify their shift away from literality. The meaning of Richard Artschwager's work remains seductively enigmatic and the structure of Sol LeWitt's wall murals conceptually clear, but now we are confronted with an evolution away from strident reductivism to concerns of style and a preference for a beauty unencumbered by intellectual obligation.

The reliance on appropriation—a Pop attribute now overlayed with a canonized attitude of cultural critique—continues to engage a number of artists. Jeff Koons transforms popular objects associated with leisure and play—basketballs, fish tanks, inflatable toys, "collectibles"—into charged, precious, and strangely disquieting works that parody the spectacle of consumer lust. The question of whether authenticity, authorship, and originality are possible in a post-industrial age of recycled information remains a vexing issue for many artists. But even the most obtuse Conceptualists have unwittingly demonstrated that idiosyncrasy and identity cannot be erased. Recognizing this, artists instead choose to redefine the meaning of those old terms by challenging the premises underlying accepted standards of representation.

The paradigm of simulation, for instance, has eroded and collapsed the dichotomy between abstraction and representation by using visual language to produce a codified response. A representation of a representation becomes an abstraction. In the case of Peter Halley, we see a picture or a diagram—of prison cells, conduits, systems of circulation, transmission and reception of information—which registers as generic, geometric abstraction. Richard Prince also plays off a generic style, whether through his use of pre-existing cartoons or his arrangement of images from magazines that have a uniform "look." By rephotographing these images, he mimics the original works but further abstracts them through re-framing, cropping, and color alteration.

Photography attained a new potential with the advent of Conceptual art, which used the medium to critique representation in general and mechanical reproduction in particular. Photography's seminal position in contemporary art is demonstrated by much post-Conceptual art, such as that of Prince, Kruger, and others presented here. The team of Clegg & Guttmann refer to the history of formal portraiture from Flemish painting to corporate reports, while emphasizing the artificiality of the posed studio photograph. Tina Barney enlarges her seemingly candid photographs of the leisure class at home to make a similar point. The large-scale arrangements of photographs that the Starn Twins employ underscore the centrality of presentation in their work. They experiment with various ways of developing and manipulating the negative and composing, collaging, and framing the image. Bruce Weber's compositions, re-presenting a variety of American male prototypes, blur the separation between fine art and commercial photography to reveal the comfort of myths. In the work of these artists, photography competes successfully with the scale and impact of painting.

Contemporary culture clings to the fiction that its history is a crucial, even revolutionary one. Although we originally likened the Biennial to a salon, the connection may only be in the quantity of contemporary art it presents. Ultimately, the traditional concept of a salon—an exhibition of aesthetically related or at least philosophically empathetic artists—is antithetical to the individualism that has characterized American art since the 1950s. This is a show of separated achievements, of works isolated from one another by different visual languages, even by whole modes of perception, and seen by a correspondingly disparate audience. It is a show of artists who have taken license to invent, reinvent, and synthesize in ways that force us to consider what we want from art.

RICHARD ARMSTRONG

RICHARD MARSHALL

LISA PHILLIPS

RICHARD ARTSCHWAGER   TINA BARNEY   JUDITH BARRY

DAVID BATES   ROSS BLECKNER   LOUISE BOURGEOIS

JOHN CHAMBERLAIN   CLEGG & GUTTMANN   GEORGE CONDO

WILLEM DE KOONING   NANCY DWYER   R.M. FISCHER

LOUISE FISHMAN   ROBERT GREENE   PETER HALLEY

ROBERT HELM   NEIL JENNEY   ROBERTO JUAREZ

JEFF KOONS   JOSEPH KOSUTH   BARBARA KRUGER

ANNETTE LEMIEUX   SOL LeWITT   ROBERT LOBE

JIM LUTES   DAVID McDERMOTT AND PETER McGOUGH

STEPHEN MUELLER   BRUCE NAUMAN   NAM JUNE PAIK

IZHAR PATKIN   JUDY PFAFF   LARI PITTMAN   RICHARD PRINCE

EDWARD RUSCHA   ROBERT RYMAN   ALAN SARET

JULIAN SCHNABEL   THE STARN TWINS   DONALD SULTAN

PHILIP TAAFFE   RICHARD TUTTLE   BRUCE WEBER

GRAHAME WEINBREN AND ROBERTA FRIEDMAN   TERRY WINTERS

Two Diners, 1987

The Organ of Cause and Effect III, 1986

RICHARD ARTSCHWAGER

Dinner (Two), 1986

The Birthday Cake, 1986

TINA BARNEY

The Card Party, 1986

The Reception, 1985

Echo, 1986
Installation at The Museum of Modern Art, New York

First and Third, 1986

Kingfisher, 1985

Red Moon, 1986

DAVID BATES

Catfish Moon, 1986

Twelve Nights, 1986

ROSS BLECKNER

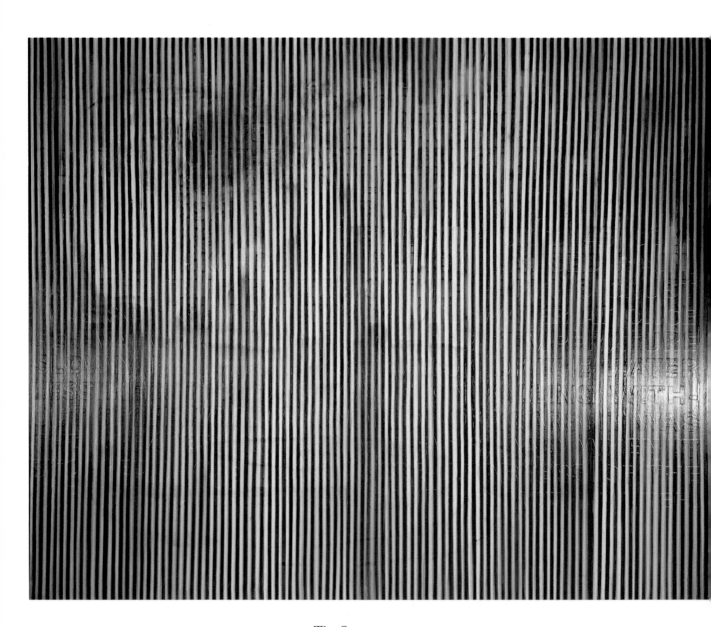

The Oceans, 1984–86

Untitled, 1985

LOUISE BOURGEOIS

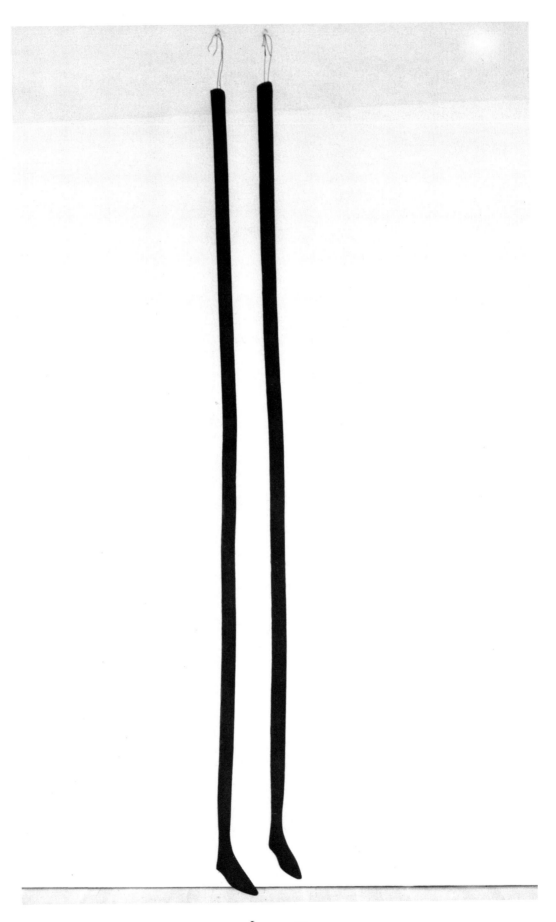

Legs, 1986

Nature Study, 1986

LOUISE BOURGEOIS

Nature Study, 1986

Iceberg, 1986

First Dance of the Trees, 1986 (two views)

The Financiers, 1986

The Gallery Proprietesses, 1986

CLEGG & GUTTMANN

Corporate Music, 1985

Black Insect, 1986

GEORGE CONDO

Dancing to Miles, 1985–86

Girl with the Purple Dress, 1986

WILLEM DE KOONING

Untitled XII, 1986

Untitled XVIII, 1986

NANCY DWYER

Coming Up Next, 1986

Your Name, 1986

Snap, Crackle, Pop, 1986

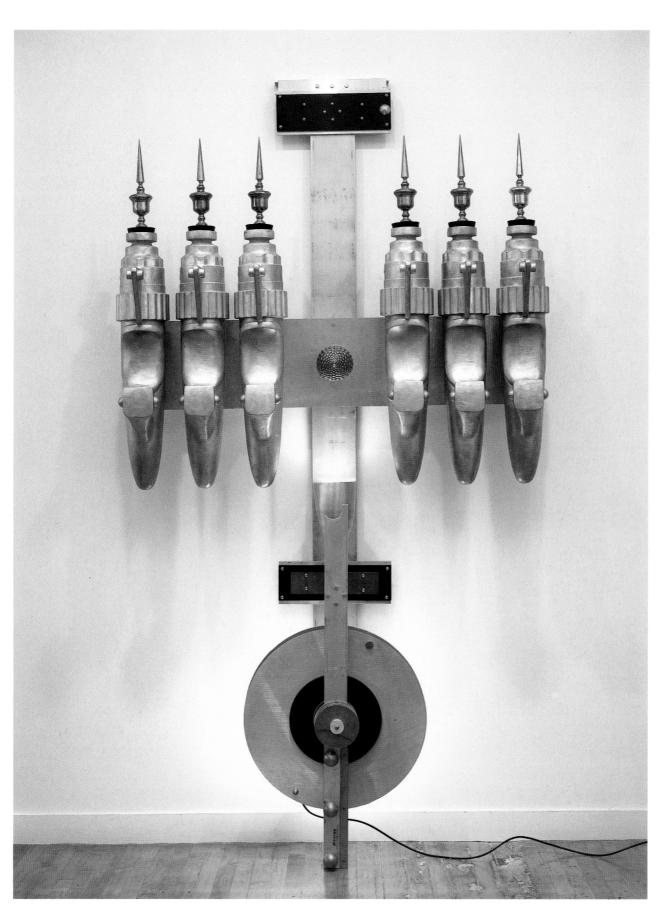

Northstar, 1986

LOUISE FISHMAN

Smuggler's Notch, 1986

Refiner's Fire, 1985

LOUISE FISHMAN

Ida's Special, 1986

The Wedding, 1985

ROBERT GREENE

Another Always, 1986

Private Thoughts, 1986

PETER HALLEY

Three Sectors, 1986

Blue Cell with Triple Conduit, 1986

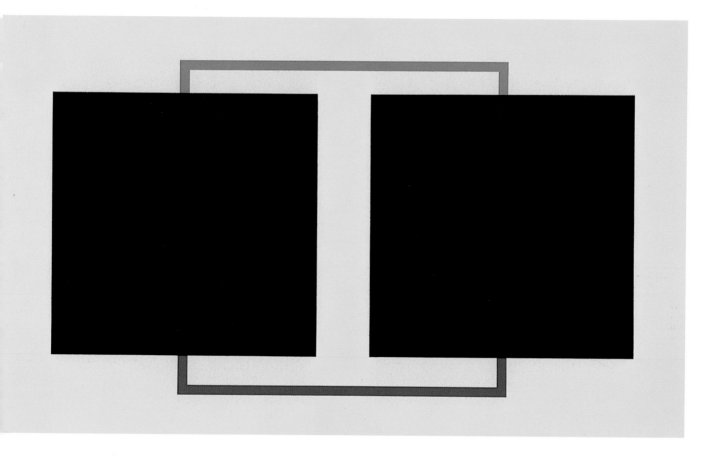

Two Cells with Circulating Conduit, 1985

ROBERT HELM

Night Window, 1986

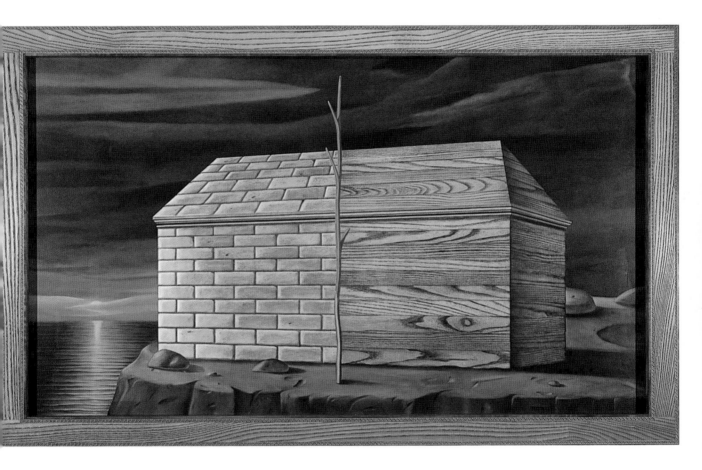

Word by Word, 1986

ROBERT HELM

Falling Hour, 1986

Venus from North America, 1979–87

Atmosphere, 1975–85

ROBERTO JUAREZ

Off-Shore Drilling, 1986

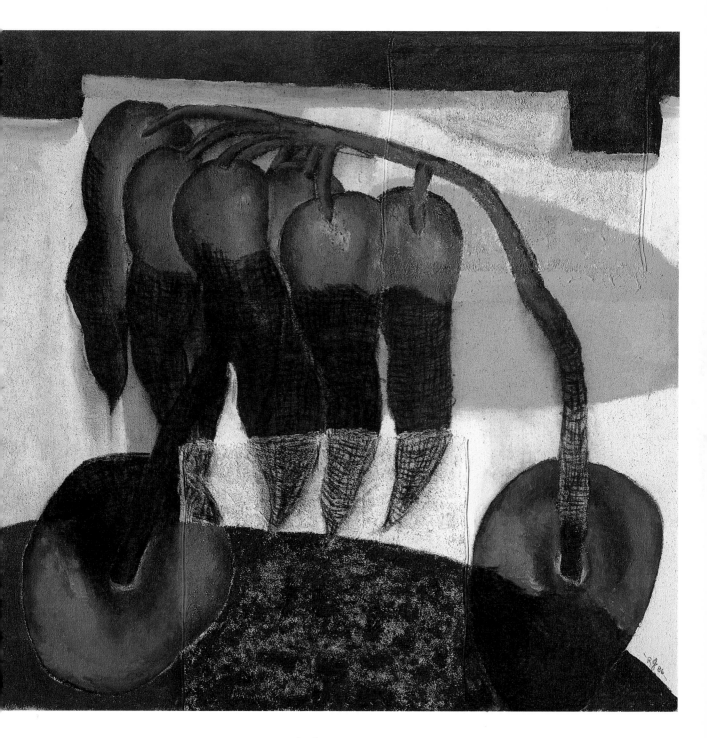

Applepeppers, 1986

ROBERTO JUAREZ

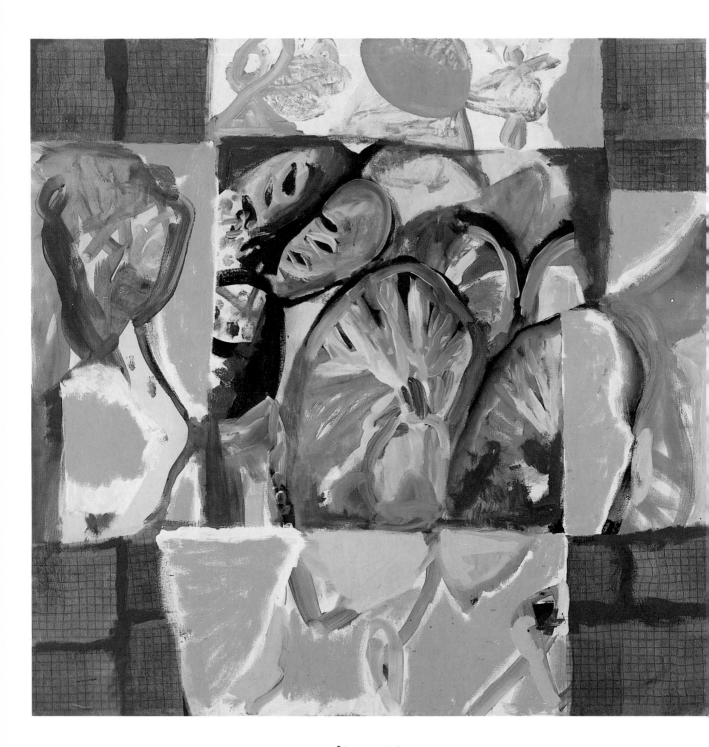

Lima, 1986

One Ball Total Equilibrium Tank, 1985

Two Ball 50-50 Tank, 1985

Rabbit, 1986

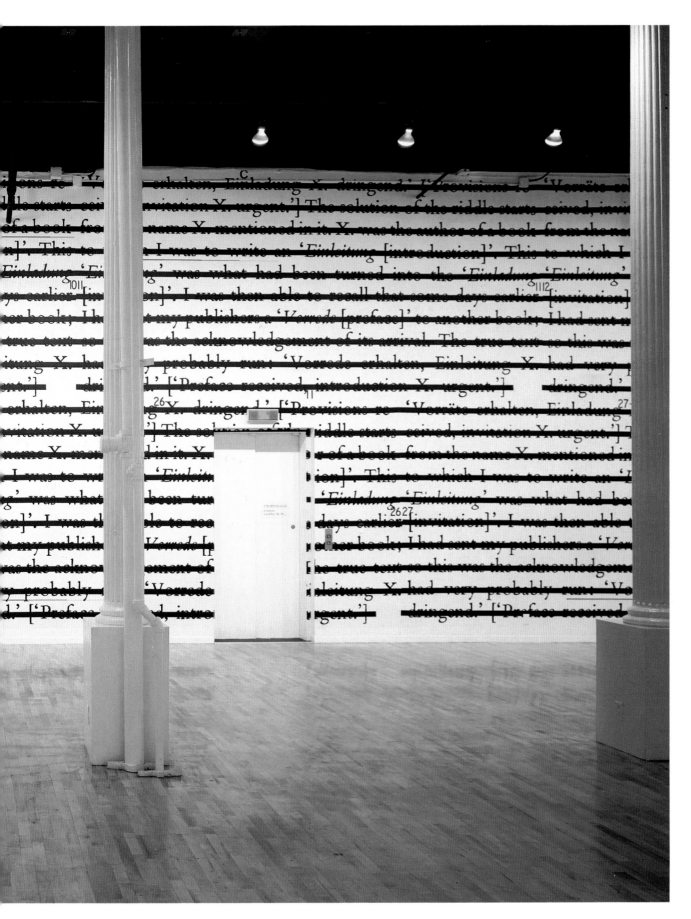

Zero & Not, 1986
Installation at Leo Castelli Gallery, New York

(6) The effects that can be produced by personal reference can also be seen in the following example, reported by Jung (1907, 52):

'A Herr Y. fell in love with a lady; but he met with no success, and shortly afterwards she married a Herr X. Thereafter, Herr Y., in spite of having known Herr X. for a long time and even having business dealings with him, forgot his name over and over again, so that several times he had to enquire what it was from other people when he wanted to correspond with Herr X.'

The motivation of the forgetting is however more transparent in this case than in the preceding ones that fall within the constellation of personal reference. Here the forgetting seems a direct consequence of Herr Y.'s antipathy to his more fortunate rival; he wants to know nothing about him: 'never thought of shall he be.'[2]

Word, Sentence, Paragraph (Z. & N.), 1986

Untitled (Worth Every Penny), 1987

BARBARA KRUGER

Untitled (In Space No One Can Hear You Scream), 1987

Untitled (I Shop Therefore I Am), 1987

ANNETTE LEMIEUX

Curious Child, 1986

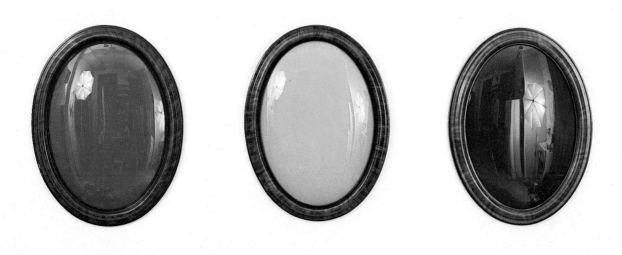

Showing One's Colors, 1986

ANNETTE LEMIEUX

Homecoming, 1985

Truncated Pyramid, 1986
Installation at The Drawing Center, New York

Multiple Pyramids, 1986
Installation at John Weber Gallery, New York

ROBERT LOBE

Facial Structure, 1986 (in progress)

Killer Hill C.W., 1985

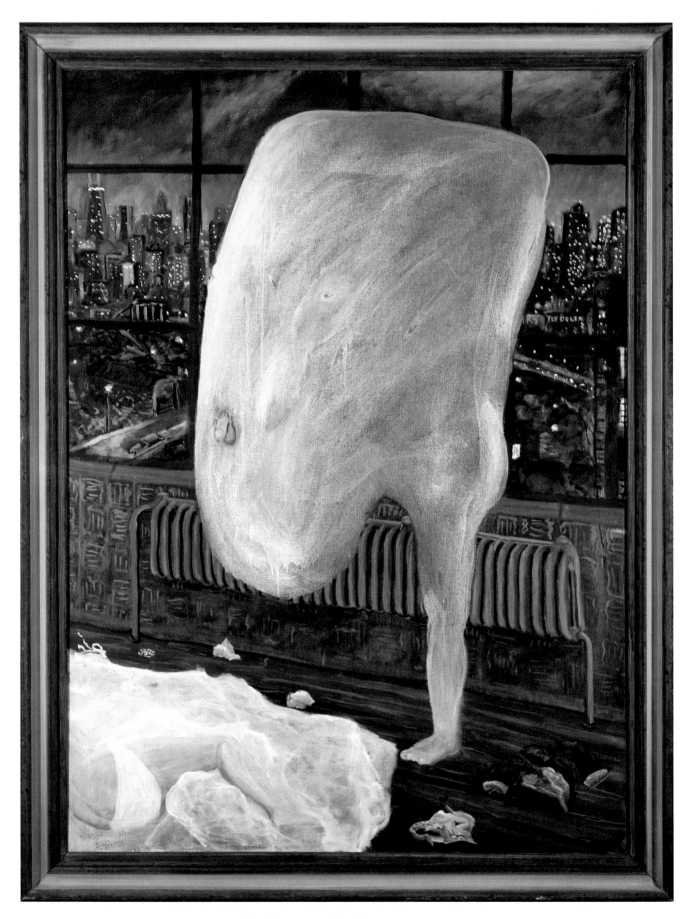

The Evening of My Disfunction, 1985

Field Day, 1986

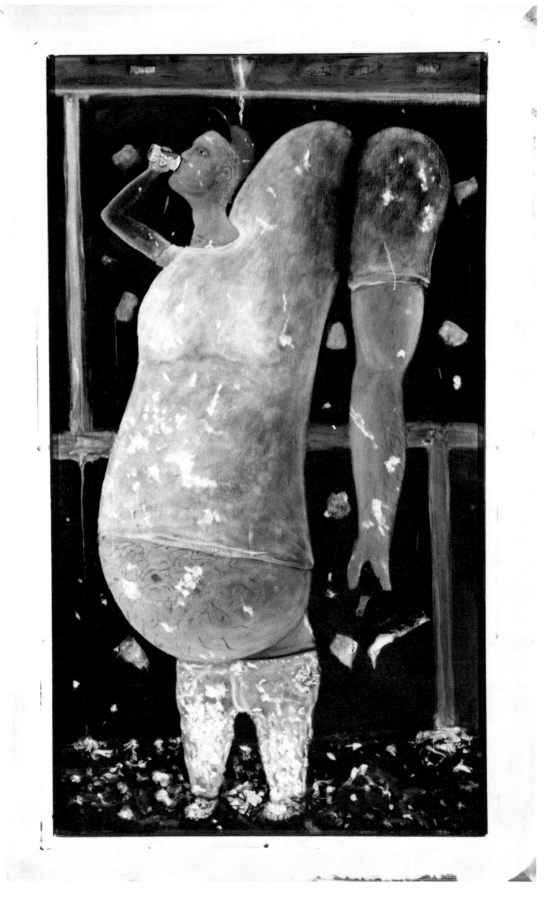

The Dry Waller, 1985

Rub-a-Dub-Dub... Three Boys... and One Tub, 1937, 1986

The Big Show, 1928, 1986

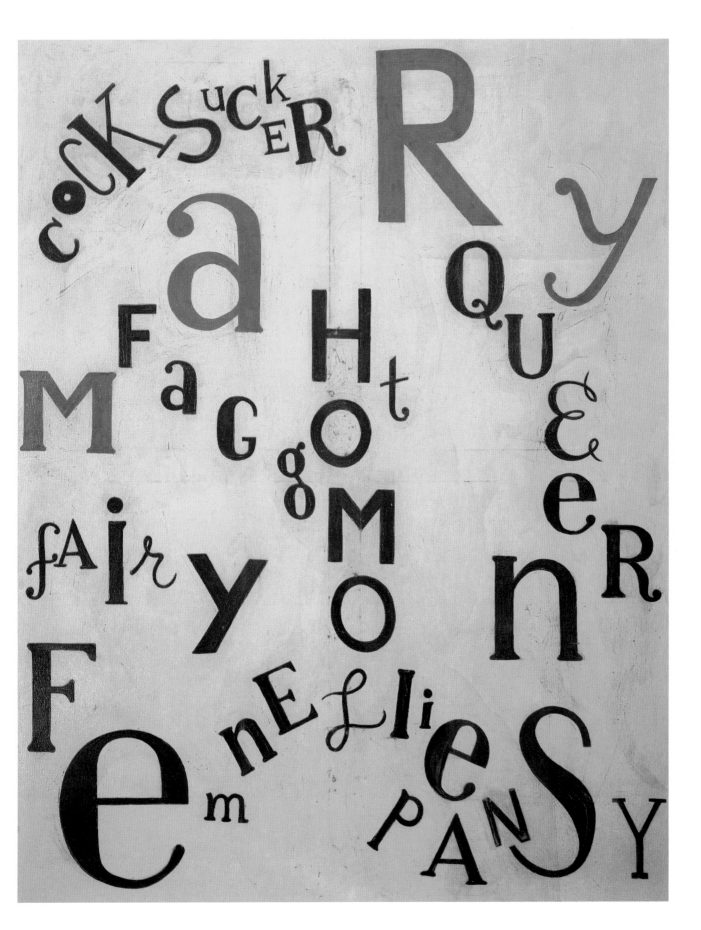

A Friend of Dorothy, 1943, 1986

STEPHEN MUELLER

St. George Lycabettus, 1986

Rushing Up Portofino, 1986

STEPHEN MUELLER

Radio Monaco, 1986

The Krefeld Piece: Hanged Man, 1985

BRUCE NAUMAN

The Krefeld Piece: Good Boy/Bad Boy, 1985

The Krefeld Piece: Good Boy/Bad Boy, 1985

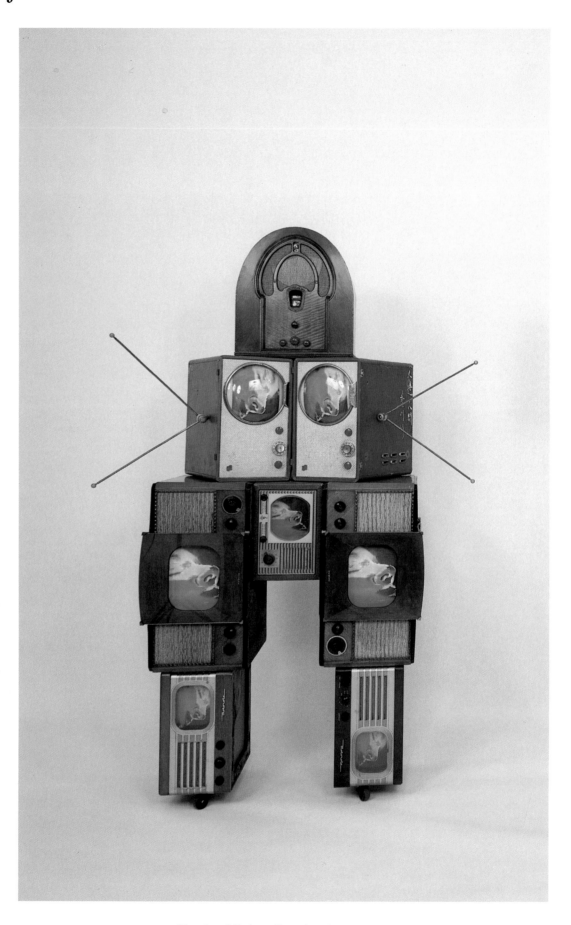

Family of Robot: Grandmother, 1986

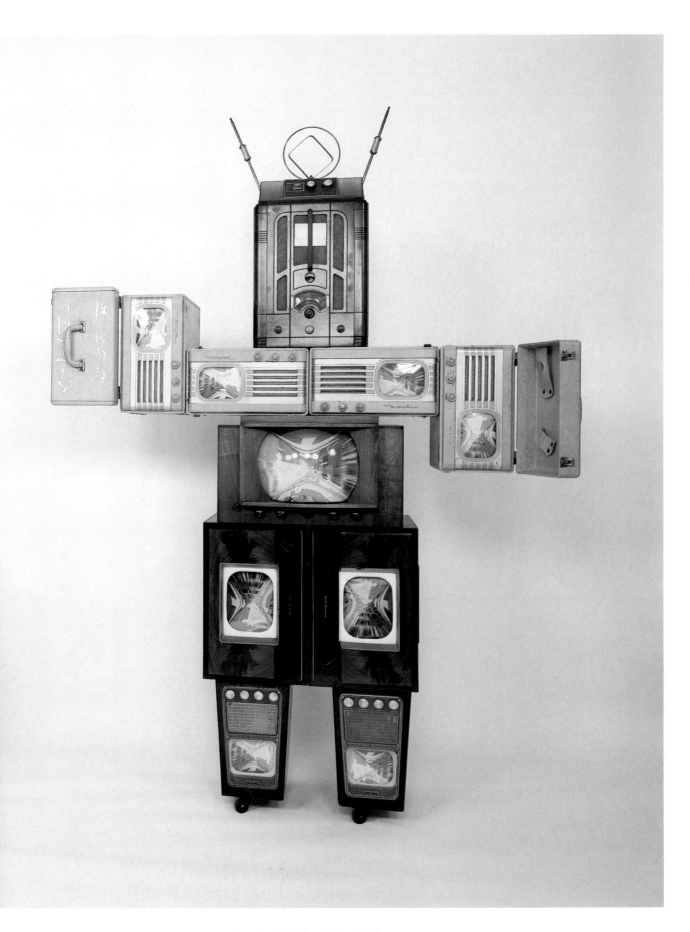

Family of Robot: Grandfather, 1986

The Black Paintings: White Ghost, 1985–86 (detail)

The Black Paintings: Night, 1985–86 (detail)

IZHAR PATKIN

The Black Paintings: Dawn, 1985–86 (detail)

Wasco, 1986

JUDY PFAFF

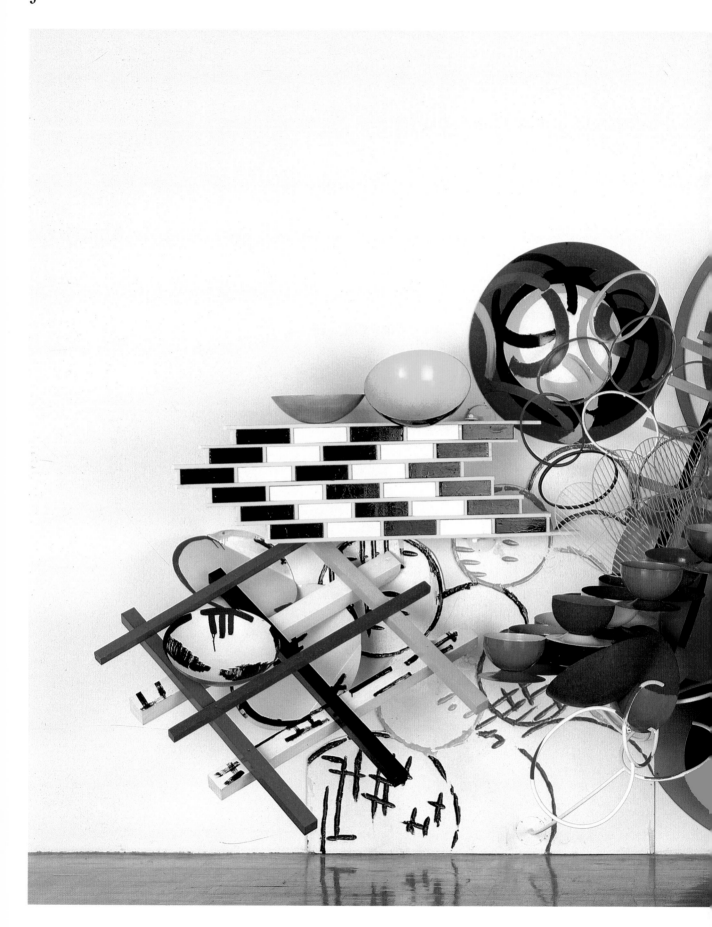

Supermercado, 1986

LARI PITTMAN

Reason to Rebuild, 1986

Out of the Frost, 1986

LARI PITTMAN

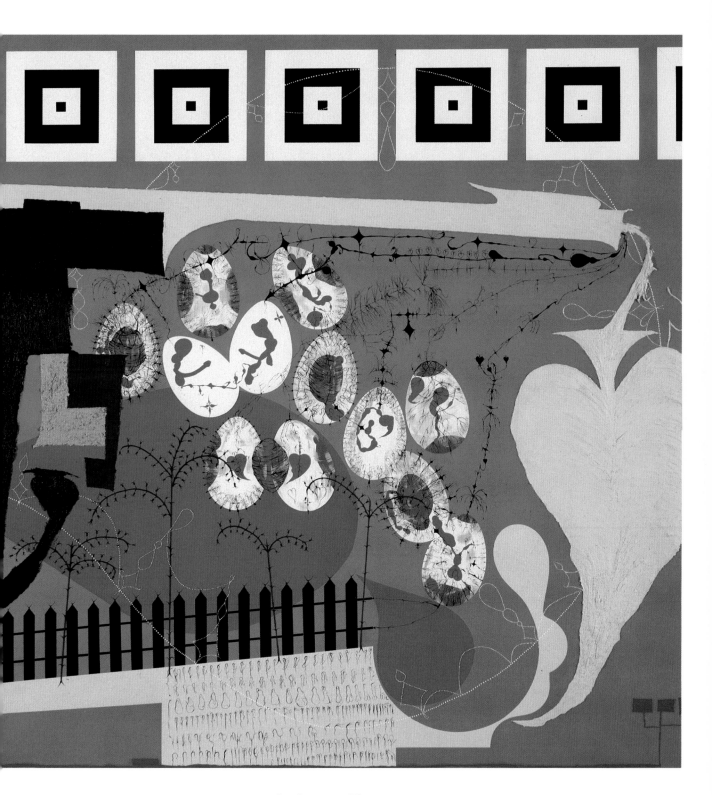

An American Place, 1986

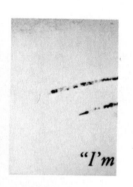

Untitled (Joke), 1986

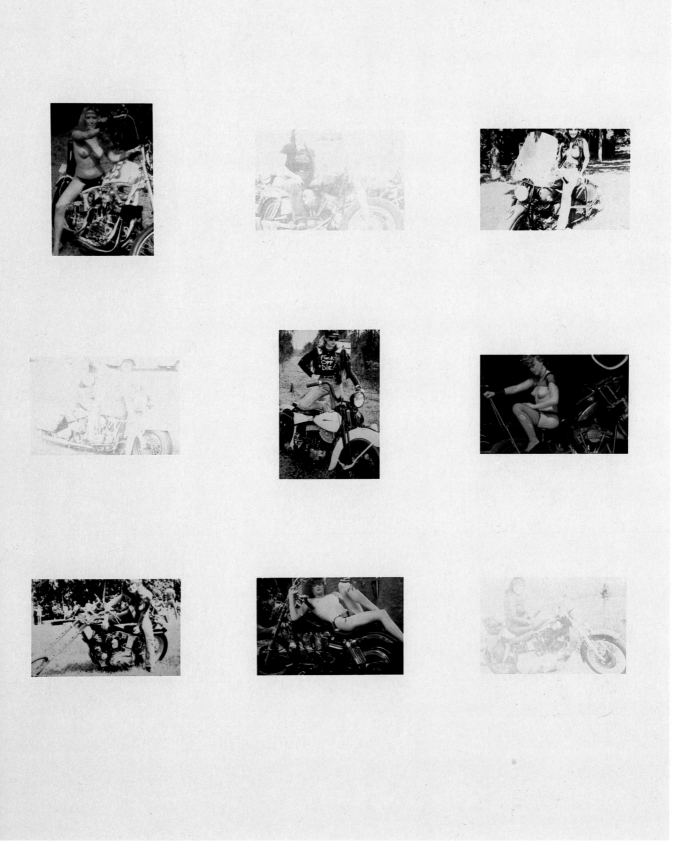

Live Free or Die, 1986

RICHARD PRINCE

Tell Me Everything, 1986

The Uncertain Trail, 1986

EDWARD RUSCHA

Name, Address, Phone, 1986

ROBERT RYMAN

Reference, 1985

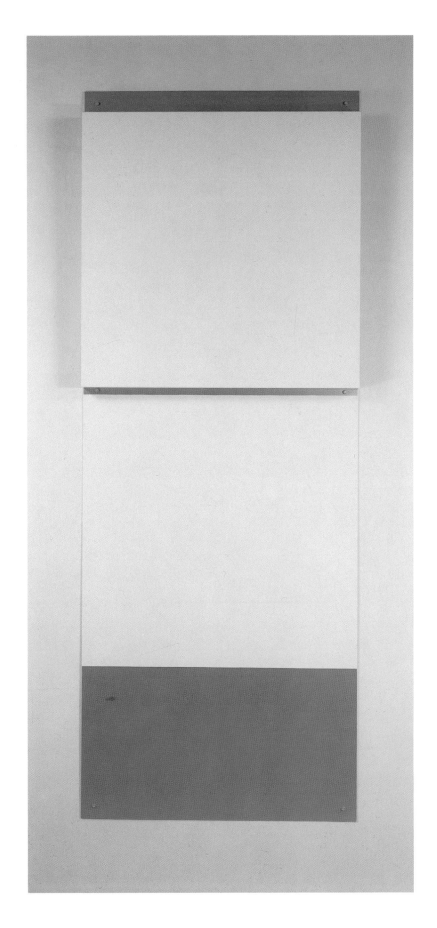

Charter, 1985

ROBERT RYMAN

Century, 1985

Alchemicomania, 1986

ALAN SARET

Chosen Women, 1986

Mimi, 1986

JULIAN SCHNABEL

Virtue, 1986

THE STARN TWINS

Mark Morrisroe, 1985–86

Double Stark Portrait in Swirl, 1985–86

Christ (Stretched), 1985–86

DONALD SULTAN

Detroit Oct 31 1986, 1986

Three Apples Three Pears and a Lemon Dec 6 1986, 1986

DONALD SULTAN

Veracruz Nov 18 1986, 1986

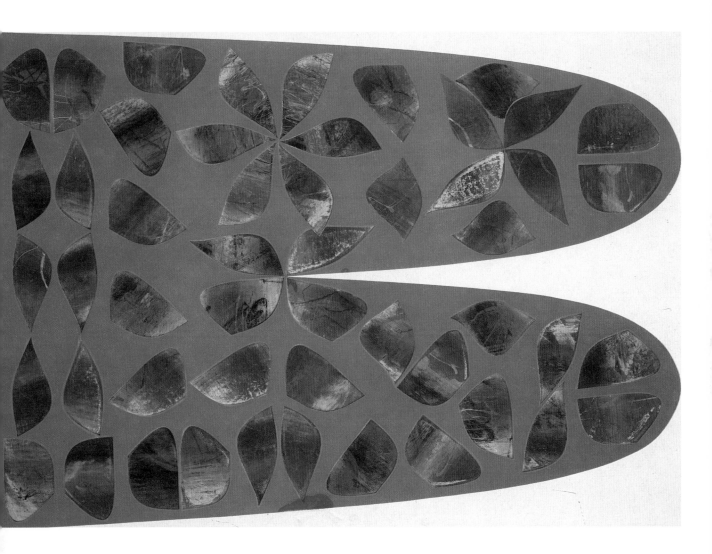

Nativity (Red, White), 1986

Quad Cinema, 1986

Yellow, Grey, 1986

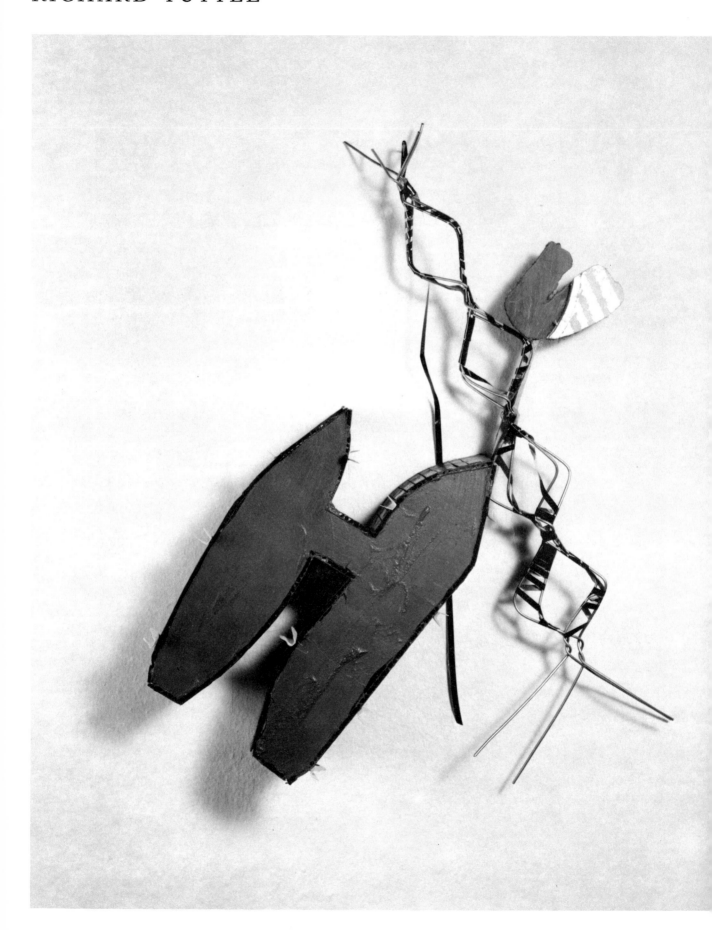

Orange Blue Yellow, 1986

Silver Mercury, 1986

Yellow "V" Against Brown, 1986

Karch "Special K" Kiraly, U.S. Olympic Volleyball Player, New York City, 1985

BRUCE WEBER

David at 29 Palms Inn, Joshua Tree, 1986

BRUCE WEBER

Chris Isaak in Limo, New York City, 1985

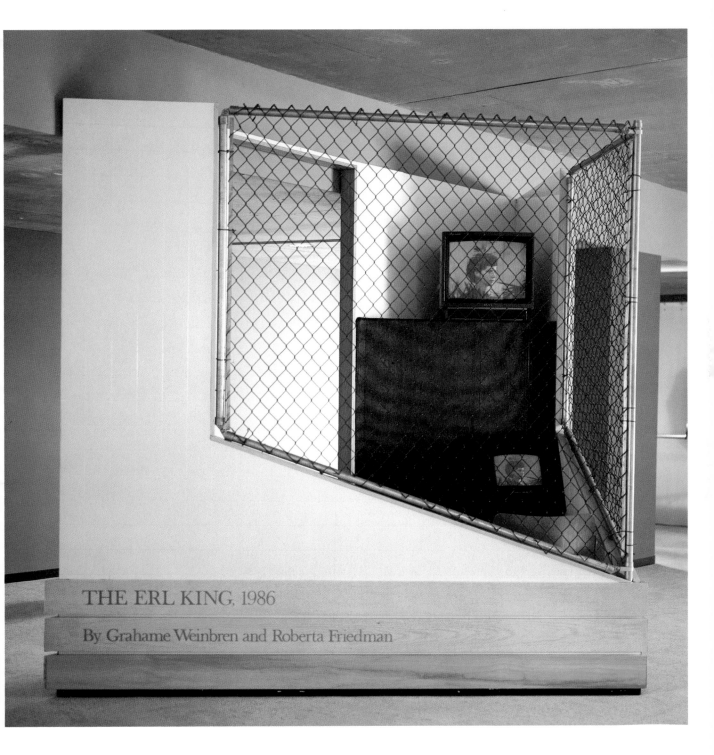

The Erl King, 1986
Installation at The Museum of Contemporary Art, Los Angeles

Pitch Lake, 1985

Asphaltum, 1986

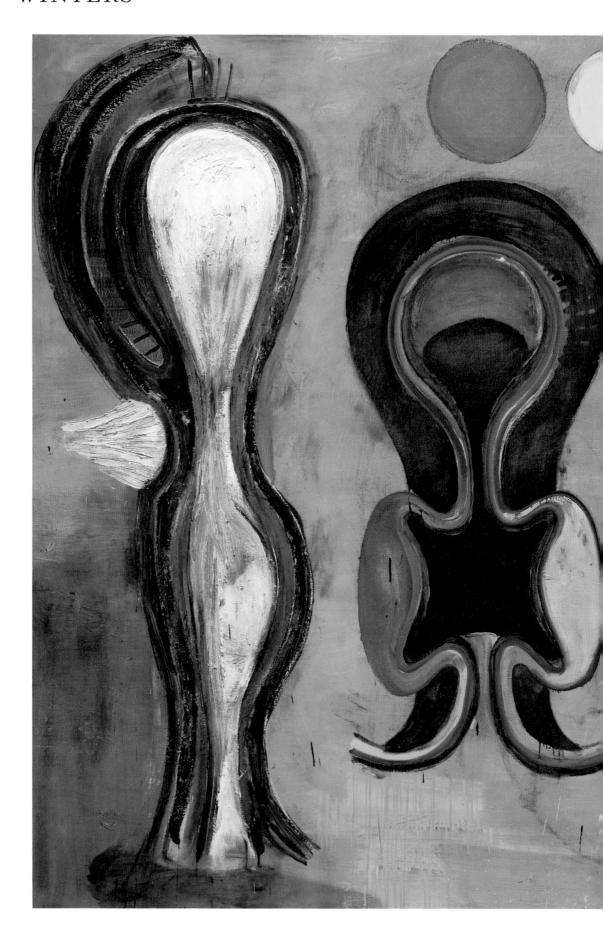

Dumb Compass, 1985

INTRODUCTION TO FILM AND VIDEO

THE 1987 BIENNIAL demonstrates the vitality of independent film and video today through the work of established and emerging artists. The exhibition surveys the variety of styles, forms, and genres that constitutes contemporary media arts. In addition to the four artists represented on the gallery floors alongside painting, sculpture, and photography, the Biennial features the work of fifteen film and fifteen video artists in the second-floor Film and Video Gallery.

The selection focuses on techniques and approaches that are shared by film and video artists. These include the narrative mode—the construction of stories through acting, sets, and written texts; the documentary genre, which represents social reality through the recorded image; the avant-garde use of abstract and image-processing techniques that explore new forms of image making; and animation, where hand-drawn and pixilated combinations of shots are worked into abstract and representational sequences. The 1987 film and video selection also investigates feminist and political issues that have become increasingly central to artists, along with more formal issues that relate to the stylistic history of film and video art.

The incorporation of video into sculpture and installation projects has been an important part of video art's history. Nam June Paik, a key figure in that history, is represented in the Biennial with two video sculptures, *Grandmother* and *Grandfather*, both made in 1986. These works refer to Paik's 1963 *Robot K–456*, a remote-controlled, humanoid form fashioned out of wire and metal. Paik included this robot in Fluxus performances, such as in Karlheinz Stockhausen's *Originale*, and in Fluxus street actions here and abroad. In the two recent works, he has created witty and compelling figures out of vintage television sets, which play a videotape created for these pieces. The installation form of video is also explored in Judith Barry's *First and Third*, in which a video image of a person's face is projected onto an interior stone wall. With a voice-over narrative about political interrogation, the faces appear as charged specters of the terror and reality of political repression. This work follows from Barry's earlier installations and videotapes that examined the transformation of public spaces by consumerism. The installation by Grahame Weinbren and Roberta Friedman, *The Erl King*, employs a highly sophisticated interactive video disk system to create a compelling and multidimensional narrative based on Schubert's song of the same title. The viewer manipulates and changes the constructed narratives and images by touching the monitor's screen. Weinbren and Friedman thus exploit new technology to shape a contemporary means of storytelling and image making.

The independent feature film, a format in which new ideas about narrative and representation are explored, has become one of the most visible and important currents in the art of film over the past two years. One of its foremost artists is Yvonne Rainer. Her latest film, *The Man Who Envied Women* (1985), insistently thwarts viewers' expectations of plot and character development and, in the process, exposes what she perceives as the patriarchal roots of narrative cinema—the traditional male-dominated point of view that determines the representation of the woman's place within the film narrative. Rainer also probes with wit and insight the lives of the intellectual and the artist as social and political beings. The film employs a number of jolting disruptions to conventional expectations: two actors play the male lead and they directly address the audience; inferior, often grainy black-and-white footage is mixed with seamless editing; and scenes with dramatic action are intercut with voice-over deconstructions of the ideology of advertising and photography. These are not mere formal devices but, drawing on feminist theory, new ways of considering cinematic meaning and spectatorship.

James Benning, another key figure in the history of the American independent film, has lately moved from purely visual, structural short films to longer works that construct narrative meaning out of image and voice. The recent films, including *Landscape Suicide* (1986), are both autobiographical and provocative meditations on American culture and society. *Landscape Suicide* juxtaposes landscape images with a series of reenacted testimonies by two murderers—a youth who stabbed a teenage girl in a California suburb, and a deranged Wisconsin man who brutally killed a female neighbor. Benning metaphorically relates each crime to its specific locale. Place becomes the condition that creates the tragedies which inhabit it. Juxtaposing the testimonies of personal destruction with imagery, Benning's cinematography subtly evokes violence, anguish, and death. *Landscape Suicide* is both a physical and mental landscape whose subtext is the artist's struggle to comprehend the world we live in.

Many of the new narrative feature films in the independent cinema eliminate the storytelling conventions that the artists regard as superfluous to a real understanding of the individual in today's social world. Rachel Reichman's *The Riverbed* (1986), in its lyrical use of black-and-white photography, evokes a dream world in which a drifter and a family he encounters act out their desires within a distinctly American landscape. This exploitation of the subconscious within the narrative extends to Nina Menkes' *Magdalena Viraga* (1986), a harsh and brutal scenario of sexual oppression. The principal character, a prostitute, becomes objectified as male society controls and manipulates her body. Although minimal in its overt action, *Magdalena Viraga* makes the real more vivid through surreality. Along with Yvonne Rainer, Reichman and Menkes propose a revision of the male-dominated, cinematic narrative through powerful symbols and characterizations.

An unconventional approach to narrative also characterizes the short film. With great invention and innovation, the independent narrative short film telescopes into a few minutes what we expect to see developed at greater length. Ernest Marrero and Susan Kouguell's *Before the Rise of Premonition* (1985) constructs its scenes around a family in which the parents act out before their children taunting rehearsals of their disintegrating relationship. Kouguell and Marrero skillfully render the actions ambiguous through an erotic tension heightened by the stylized setting and lighting of the scenes. Leandro Katz's *The Visit* (1986) constructs the narrative with sound effects and a visual style evocative of *film noir*, the dramatically stylized and acted melodramas of the 1940s. As the film unfolds, the action shifts to different places and characters appear and disappear as events propel the action forward in a seamless and apparently logical sequence. In fact, as meaning and belief are constantly questioned, the story appears to turn upon itself like a Möbius strip.

The Dream Screen (1986) by Stephanie Beroes focuses on the life and myth of film star Louise Brooks. Intercut into *The Dream Screen* are scenes from G.W. Pabst's *Pandora's Box* (1929), starring Brooks as Lulu, a contemporary femme fatale, and a Brooks look-alike who talks about her relationship with her mother, in conjunction with voice-over readings from Brooks' autobiography. These three central figures reflect one another and become a means through which to examine the place of the woman in film history and in the cultural imagination. Myth in the form of the fairy tale is the subject of Ericka Beckman's *Cinderella* (1986). Beckman reenacts the story in a foundry suffused with an aura of gold. The gigantic sets parody the process of industrial production, as Cinderella keeps the foundry clean while pursuing the prince. The choreographed action and exaggerated gestures create a compelling mime of the story as a contemporary tale of greed.

Trinh T. Minh-ha's *Naked Spaces: Living Is Round* (1985) challenges traditional Western methods of representing "other" cultures of the world. These methods cast the filmmaker as the authority who interprets third world culture through Western languages and codes of image making. Trinh T. Minh-ha, recording the morphology of African architecture, constantly questions her position as filmmaker by employing different written and visual languages of representation. She undercuts the presumed authority of the film's point of view by moving the camera and editing the sequences in ways that counter the formulas of documentary filmmaking. *Naked Spaces* confirms the doubts raised by contemporary ethnographers about the authority of "writing culture" by actually using these doubts to interpret and practice filmmaking.

There is within the history of the independent film a long tradition of artists who have incorporated found footage—footage from abandoned or forgotten films—and given it new life through the process of juxtaposition. In *The Family Album* (1986), Alan Berliner uses found footage as well as that from his own family home movies. What emerges is an almost seamless collective image of families and individuals documenting themselves celebrating such rituals as birthdays, weddings, and picnics. The editing does not follow one family or individual, rather, the work is constructed out of different pieces of film and sound that rhythmically grow and change over time. The disjunction between soundtrack and image curiously heightens the reality and surreality of the "home movie" as a private dream.

The power of the recorded image and memory is the central concern of Ernie Gehr's and Warren Sonbert's cinema. *Signal—Germany on the Air* (1985) was shot in Berlin when Gehr was an artist-in-residence there. The silent camera frames and records the street scene in a series of static shots. Gehr's exquisite timing and sure composition, together with the editing and repetitive play of images, destabilize the ordinary-looking scene and make it a place of memory—a sense heightened by the sound track recorded off the air. Warren Sonbert's *The Cup and the Lip* (1986) continues his series of filmic diaries composed of sequences and shots recorded during his travels. One of Sonbert's most striking color films, *The Cup and the Lip* presents a portrait of people at ease as private individuals and at attention as representatives of state. In its personal way, it is a political text reflecting on authority.

The abstract animated film has a distinguished place in the history of independent film. Unlike cartoon drawing, which mimics the cinematic point of view in creating characters and a realistic or narrative space, the hand-made, drawn, and collage films of the avant-garde treat graphics as artificial constructs. Paul Glabicki's *Object Conversation* (1985), a virtuoso display of abstract images, creates a visual and verbal dialogue around objects whose meaning constantly changes through a playful and witty manipulation of lines and shapes.

Barbara Hammer's *Optic Nerve* (1985) is a powerful personal reflection on family and aging. Hammer employs filmed footage which, through optical printing and editing, is layered and manipulated to create a compelling meditation on her visit to her mother in a nursing home. The sense of sight becomes a constantly evolving process of reseeing images retrieved from the past and fused into the eternal present of the projected image. Hammer has lent a new voice to the long tradition of personal meditation in the avant-garde of the American independent cinema.

It seems particularly appropriate in the 1987 Biennial to exhibit films together with videotapes in the Film and Video Gallery. In this way, their shared concerns—the genres of narrative, documentary, avant-garde, and animation—become evident. Their differences, however, are in part shaped by the electronic basis of video and its forms of image making: the manipulation of content and the formal joining of images through image processing and electronic editing both on the low and high tech ends of production.

Bill Viola's *I Do Not Know What It Is I Am Like* (1986) reads like a phenomenology of perception as the artist meditates on the world and how we see and respond to it as a physical and spiritual environment. The eye of the artist becomes that of the camera, partly facilitated through the real-time image-making process of video, thus positing a visionary catalogue of images and sensations. We move, through its five parts, from still-life interiors, to images of animals in nature, to landscapes and Indian fire-walking rituals. That "eye" is also the self, the "I" of the artist who constructs his phenomenological inquiry into sensation and perception as a cross-cultural reference to other ways of seeing and thinking.

The relationship of language to image has been at the center of Gary Hill's work. His videotape *URA ARU (the backside exists)* (1985–86), produced while he was an artist-in-residence in Japan, treats a selection of Japanese words as palindromes, words that read the same backward or forward. In the tape, which consists of a series of visual-verbal *haiku*, Hill employs great economy of action and technique as the printed word, moving through each scene, echoes the spoken word. In inscribing language in the narrative space, Hill places language and image in a dialectical relationship.

Hans Breder's *My TV Dictionary: The Drill* (1986) and *My TV Dictionary: The Helicopter* (1986) explore the relationship of the home viewer to commercial television. These works, part of a series, use footage from commercial programs, recorded off the television screen, which is then edited into a montage that reveals the violent and sexist subtext of commercial television. This re-edited, found footage exposes the dream text of nightmarish violence that lies between the lines of television programming.

Artists have both implicitly and explicitly rejected the paradigm of commercial television in videotapes that critique and reveal its socio-cultural ideology. Sherry Millner's *Scenes from the Micro War* (1986) creates a satiric narrative of the nuclear family consumed by the rhetoric of militarism while acting out fantasies of Rambo-esque survivalists. Here the rhetoric of power delivered on television and in the print media is turned on itself, as Millner proposes a solution both to domestic and international issues through a strong combat elite force or "contra" policy. Martha Rosler's *If It's Too Bad to Be True, It Could Be DISINFORMATION* (1985) takes network news reports directly off the television and interrupts them with electronic interference, blocking out and disrupting the flow of "information." The static breakup of the image creates a literal metaphor for the disinformation that creeps into media newscasts in the guise of objective reporting. Rosler's videotape becomes a vivid emblem of the impact and influence of the mass media. Joan Braderman's *Joan Does Dynasty* (1986) literally places the artist into the serial melodrama *Dynasty* through the technique of video keying. Braderman's running commentary and her physical interruption of the show's narrative constitute a witty and deflating critique of that program. She reveals the commodification of women through objects, clothes, and sex, as well as the frustration of efforts to counteract the power of commercial television. Yet Braderman has inventively done just that by placing herself within the "text" and exposing the show and television itself as a means of merchandizing a way of life.

Video artists have appropriated a variety of legends and artifacts to explore how culture represents itself in history and myth. Steve Fagin's *The Amazing Voyage of Gustave Flaubert and Raymond Roussel* (1986) audaciously weaves together texts by Flaubert and Roussel, along with images by Marcel Duchamp. Through performance and dialogue, these appropriated literary languages and images playfully exhume the pre-modernist and modernist texts as a kind of visual "language machine," to use Michel Foucault's term for Roussel's Surrealist texts. The appropriation of classical myth is the basis of Bruce and Norman Yonemoto's *Kappa* (1986). The Kappa is a mythological Japanese figure who pursues young women and yearns to be part of a society from which he is excluded. Anarchic and archaic, the Kappa is still a popular myth in Japan and has even been used to promote a popular soft drink. The Yonemotos have a particular interest in the fetishizing habits of popular culture. Here they use the Kappa, played by visual artist Mike Kelley, as a means to satirize the values and qualities of contemporary life. Dan Graham's *Rock My Religion* (1986) traces the history of rock and roll in terms of a proposed relationship to religion in American culture. Through image and interpretive text, Graham links rock and roll's messianic and often ecstatic appeal to young people to the fervor of religious groups from the Shakers to Southern Baptists.

The personal documentary has an important place in the history of independent video. Skip Sweeney has been one of its leading figures and his videotape *My Mother Married Wilbur Stump* (1985) is an extraordinary portrait of his mother and the man she married after the death of Skip's father. Through home movies and interviews, Sweeney builds a marvelously witty portrait of his mother and Wilbur Stump that explores the family's interrelationships. A companion piece to his earlier work *My Father Sold Studebakers*, the tape is an outstanding example of *video verité*, where the artist establishes a dialogue with his subject through the camera. Juan Downey's *J.S. Bach* (1986) is also a personal documentary. One of his series of videotapes which, through the techniques of video, investigates the semiotics of culture and society, *J.S. Bach* begins with the artist's reflection on the death of his mother. Although also about the music and life of Bach, it is hardly a conventional portrait of the composer.

The special techniques of video image processing have always been important aspects of video art. Today, when a whole set of "special effects" techniques has been devised for commercial purposes, it is important to identify work that does not use these techniques as effects but as the vocabulary for a new visual language. Matthew Schlanger's *Lumpy Banger* (1986) and *Before the Flood* (1985) reject the rigid digital symmetries of many image-processed techniques, creating instead an intertextual print and painterly form that is specifically video in its movement and quality. Peer Bode's *Blind Fields* (1985) and *Animal Migrations* (1985) use found footage, abstract images, music, and text to extend image processing into new metaphors for the transformed and changing image. Bode's style charts a refreshing change in the relationship of the image to sound and text. In his work, sound and text support and play with the meaning of the image rather than illustrate it. Shalom Gorewitz, one of the leading figures in image-processing video, further extends his exploration of language and image relationships in *Run* (1986) through multilayered, colorized, and constantly shifting abstract and representational images.

Nineteen eighty-seven is the fifth year that both film and video are fully represented in the Biennial. During that time, these two media have been affected by enormous changes in the economy and technologies of production, distribution, and exhibition. The work presented here confirms that independent film and video art not only have appropriated these technological revisions, but are using them to engage in the aesthetic and ideological concerns of today.

JOHN G. HANHARDT

ERICKA BECKMAN   JAMES BENNING   ALAN BERLINER

STEPHANIE BEROES   PEER BODE   JOAN BRADERMAN

HANS BREDER   JUAN DOWNEY   STEVE FAGIN

ERNIE GEHR   PAUL GLABICKI   SHALOM GOREWITZ

DAN GRAHAM   BARBARA HAMMER   GARY HILL

LEANDRO KATZ   ERNEST MARRERO AND SUSAN KOUGUELL

NINA MENKES   SHERRY MILLNER   YVONNE RAINER

RACHEL REICHMAN   MARTHA ROSLER   MATTHEW SCHLANGER

WARREN SONBERT   SKIP SWEENEY   TRINH T. MINH-HA

BILL VIOLA   BRUCE AND NORMAN YONEMOTO

ERICKA BECKMAN

Cinderella, 1986

Landscape Suicide, 1986

ALAN BERLINER

The Family Album, 1986

The Dream Screen, 1986

Blind Fields, 1985

Joan Does Dynasty, 1986

HANS BREDER

My TV Dictionary: The Drill, 1986

J.S. Bach, 1986

STEVE FAGIN

The Amazing Voyage of Gustave Flaubert and Raymond Roussel, 1986

Signal—Germany on the Air, 1985

Object Conversation, 1985

Run, 1986

DAN GRAHAM

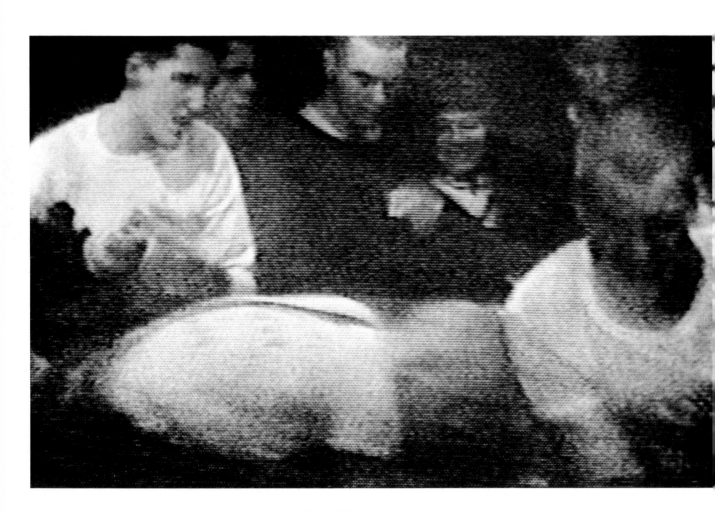

Rock My Religion, 1986

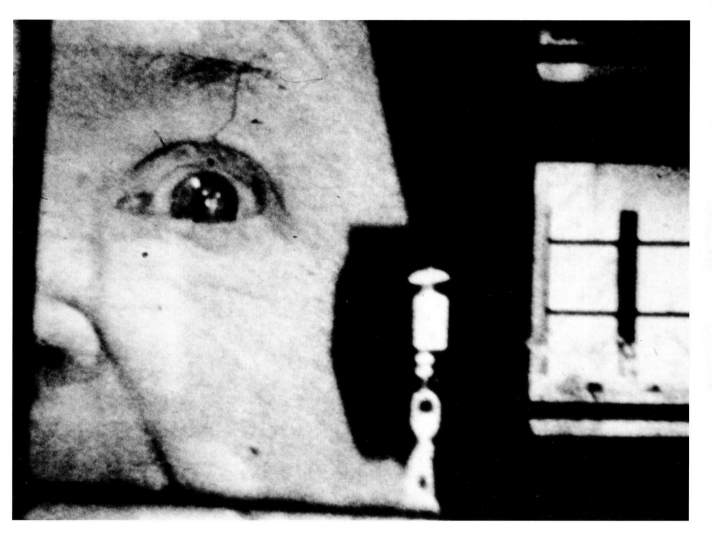

Optic Nerve, 1985

URA ARU (the backside exists), 1985–86

The Visit, 1986

Before the Rise of Premonition, 1985

Magdalena Viraga: The Story of a Red Sea Crossing, 1986

Scenes from the Micro War, 1986

The Man Who Envied Women, 1985

RACHEL REICHMAN

The Riverbed, 1986

If It's Too Bad to Be True, It Could Be DISINFORMATION, 1985

Lumpy Banger, 1986

The Cup and the Lip, 1986

SKIP SWEENEY

My Mother Married Wilbur Stump, 1985

Naked Spaces: Living Is Round, 1985

BILL VIOLA

I Do Not Know What It Is I Am Like, 1986

Kappa, 1986

PAINTING SCULPTURE PHOTOGRAPHY

RICHARD ARTSCHWAGER

Born in Washington, D.C., 1923
Studied at Cornell University,
   Ithaca, New York (B.A., 1942)
Lives in New York

ONE-ARTIST EXHIBITIONS

1965 Leo Castelli Gallery, New York
1968 Galerie Konrad Fischer, Düsseldorf
1973 Museum of Contemporary Art,
   Chicago
1974 Daniel Weinberg Gallery,
   San Francisco
1978 Kunstverein Hamburg (traveled)
1979 Albright-Knox Art Gallery, Buffalo
   (traveled)
1980 Museum of Art, Rhode Island School
   of Design, Providence
1985 Leo Castelli Gallery, New York
   Kunsthalle Basel, Switzerland

GROUP EXHIBITIONS

1966 The Jewish Museum, New York,
   "Primary Structures"
1968 Kassel, West Germany, "Documenta 4"
1969 Kunsthalle Bern, Switzerland, "Live
   in Your Head: When Attitudes Become
   Form: Works—Concepts—Processes—
   Situations—Information" (traveled)
1970 The Museum of Modern Art,
   New York, "Information"
1974 Whitney Museum of American Art,
   New York, "American Pop Art"
1976 Whitney Museum of American Art,
   New York, "200 Years of American
   Sculpture"
1977 Institute of Contemporary Art,
   University of Pennsylvania, Philadelphia,
   "Improbable Furniture"
   Museum of Contemporary Art, Chicago,
   "A View of a Decade"
1980 Venice, Italy, "XXXIX Biennale di
   Venezia"
1981 Margo Leavin Gallery, Los Angeles,
   "Cast, Carved and Constructed"
1982 Kassel, West Germany, "Documenta 7"
1983 The Tate Gallery, London, "New Art"
1984 Donald Young Gallery, Chicago,
   "American Sculpture"
1985 Whitney Museum of American Art,
   Fairfield County, Stamford, Connecticut,
   "Affiliations: Recent Sculpture and Its
   Antecedents"

BIBLIOGRAPHY

Ammann, Jean-Christophe. *Richard
   Artschwager* (exhibition catalogue). Basel,
   Switzerland: Kunsthalle Basel, 1985.
Armstrong, Richard, Linda L. Cathcart, and
   Suzanne Delehanty. *Richard Artschwager's
   Theme(s)* (exhibition catalogue).
   La Jolla, California: La Jolla Museum
   of Contemporary Art, 1979.
Smith, Roberta. "The Artschwager
   Enigma." *Art in America*, 67 (October
   1979), pp. 92–95.
Van Bruggen, Coosje. "Richard
   Artschwager." *Artforum*, 22 (September
   1983), pp. 44-51.
Welish, Marjorie. "The Elastic Vision of
   Richard Artschwager." *Art in America*, 66
   (May-June 1978), pp. 85–87.

TINA BARNEY

Born in New York, 1945
Studied at Sun Valley Center for Arts and
   Humanities, Idaho (1976–79)
Lives in Watch Hill, Rhode Island

ONE-ARTIST EXHIBITIONS

1985 Tatistcheff and Company, New York

GROUP EXHIBITIONS

1983 The Museum of Modern Art, New
   York, "Big Pictures"
1984 The Hudson River Museum, Yonkers,
   New York, "The Lens in the Garden"
1985 Union Gallery, San Jose State
   University, California, "Humanistic
   Visions"
1986 CDS Gallery, New York, "Artists
   Choose Artists"

BIBLIOGRAPHY

Bolt, Thomas. "Tina Barney." *Arts
   Magazine,* 59 (May 1985), p. 25.
Edwards, Owen. "Summer Snapshots."
   American Photographer, 15 (September
   1985), pp. 33, 35.
Grundberg, Andy. "Big Pictures That Say
   Little." *The New York Times*, May 8, 1983,
   pp. H31, H36.

JUDITH BARRY

Born in Columbus, Ohio, 1949
Studied at the University of Florida,
   Gainesville (B.S., 1972); San Francisco
   Art Institute (1974–75); University of
   California, Berkeley (1975–78); New
   York Institute of Technology, Old
   Westbury (1984–85)
Lives in New York

ONE-ARTIST EXHIBITIONS

1977 80 Langton Street, San Francisco
1978 San Francisco Museum of
   Modern Art
1980 The Museum of Modern Art,
   New York
1982 Internationaal Cultureel Centrum,
   Antwerp
   Whitney Museum of American Art,
   New York
1984 Stichting de Appel, Amsterdam
1985 Spectacolor Board, Times Square,
   New York
1986 The Museum of Modern Art,
   New York
   New Langton Arts, San Francisco

GROUP EXHIBITIONS

1982 The Biennale of Sydney, Australia
1983 Institute of Contemporary Arts,
   London, "Scenes and Conventions,
   Artists' Architecture"
1984 Allen Memorial Art Museum,
   Oberlin, Ohio, "New Voices 4"
   The New Museum of Contemporary Art,
   New York, "Difference: On
   Representation and Sexuality"
   Walter Phillips Gallery, Banff, Alberta,
   Canada, "Social Spaces"
1985 Artists Space, New York,
   "Dark Rooms"
   Long Beach Museum of Art, California,
   "A Passage Repeated"
   The New Museum of Contemporary Art,
   New York, "The Art of Memory/The
   Loss of History"
1986 Mercer Union Gallery, Toronto,
   "Dark/Light"
   The New Museum of Contemporary Art,
   New York, "Damaged Goods: Desire
   and the Economy of the Object"

BIBLIOGRAPHY

Barry, Judith. "Building Conventions."
Real Life, Summer 1981, pp. 33–35.
———. "Casual Shopper." *Discourse*, no. 4
(Winter 1981–82), pp. 4–34.
———. "Dissenting Spaces." In Brian
Wallis, ed., *Damaged Goods: Desire and the
Economy of the Object* (exhibition
catalogue). New York: The New Museum
of Contemporary Art, 1986, pp. 46–49.
Lehman, Peter. "Video Art and Video
Games: An Interview with Judith Barry."
Wide Angle, 6 (March 1984), pp. 50–58.
London, Barbara. "Video: Its Context." In
Video by Artists 2, edited by Elke Town.
Toronto: Art Metropole, 1986, pp. 16–30.

DAVID BATES

Born in Dallas, 1952
Studied at Southern Methodist University,
Dallas (B.F.A., 1975); Independent Study
Program, Whitney Museum of American
Art, New York (1976–77); Southern
Methodist University, Dallas (M.F.A.,
1977)
Lives in Dallas

ONE-ARTIST EXHIBITIONS

1976 Allen Street Gallery, Dallas
1981 DW Gallery, Dallas
1983 Charles Cowles Gallery, New York
1984 Texas Gallery, Houston
1985 John Berggruen Gallery,
San Francisco
Charles Cowles Gallery, New York
Betsy Rosenfield Gallery, Chicago
1986 Texas Gallery, Houston

GROUP EXHIBITIONS

1978 Laguna Gloria Art Museum, Austin,
Texas, "Annual Southwest Exhibition:
Painting and Sculpture"
1983 Contemporary Arts Museum,
Houston, "American Still Life:
1945–1983"
Contemporary Arts Museum, Houston,
"Southern Fictions"
The Corcoran Gallery of Art,
Washington, D.C., "The 38th Biennial
Exhibition of Contemporary American
Painting" (traveled)
New Orleans Museum of Art, "New
Orleans Triennial"
1984 The Berkshire Museum, Pittsfield,
Massachusetts, "Aspects of New
Narrative Art" (traveled)
Museum of Art, Fort Lauderdale, "New
Narrative Painting: Selections from the
Metropolitan Museum of Art" (traveled)

BIBLIOGRAPHY

Cathcart, Linda L. *American Still Life: 1945–
1983* (exhibition catalogue). Houston:
Contemporary Arts Museum, 1983.
Handy, Ellen. "David Bates." *Arts Magazine*,
60 (December 1985), p. 117.
Henry, Gerrit. "David Bates at Charles
Cowles." *Art in America*, 71 (November
1983), pp. 225–26.
Lieberman, William. *New Narrative Painting:
Selections from the Metropolitan Museum of
Art* (exhibition catalogue). Fort
Lauderdale: Museum of Art, 1984.

ROSS BLECKNER

Born in New York, 1949.
Studied at New York University (B.A.,
1971); California Institute of the Arts,
Valencia (M.F.A., 1973)
Lives in New York

ONE-ARTIST EXHIBITIONS

1975 Cunningham Ward, New York
1976 John Doyle Gallery, Chicago
1979 Mary Boone Gallery, New York
1980 Mary Boone Gallery, New York
1981 Mary Boone Gallery, New York
1982 Galerie Patrick Verelist, Antwerp
1983 Mary Boone Gallery, New York
1984 Nature Morte Gallery, New York
1986 Mary Boone Gallery, New York
Mario Diacono Gallery, Boston

GROUP EXHIBITIONS

1975 Whitney Museum of American Art,
New York, "1975 Biennial Exhibition"
1979 Hallwalls, Buffalo, "Four Artists"
Hayward Gallery, London, "New
Painting New York"
1981 California Institute of the Arts,
Valencia, "Tenth Anniversary Exhibition"
1984 International With Monument
Gallery, New York, "Still Life with
Transaction"
Nature Morte Gallery, New York,
"Civilization and the Landscape of
Discontent"
Renaissance Society at the University of
Chicago, "The Meditative Surface"
1985 Institute of Contemporary Art,
Boston, "Currents"
The New Museum of Contemporary Art,
New York, "The Art of Memory/The
Loss of History"
Postmasters Gallery, New York,
"Paravision"

BIBLIOGRAPHY

Halley, Peter. "Ross Bleckner: Painting at
the End of History." *Arts Magazine*, 56
(May 1982), pp. 132–33.
Indiana, Gary. "Light and Death." *The
Village Voice*, February 12, 1986, p. 94.
Kuspit, Donald. "Ross Bleckner." *Artforum*,
22 (April 1984), p. 82.
Siegel, Jeanne. "Geometry Desurfacing:
Ross Bleckner, Alan Belcher, Ellen Carey,
Peter Halley, Sherrie Levine, Philip
Taaffe and James Welling." *Arts Magazine*,
60 (March 1986), pp. 26–32.

LOUISE BOURGEOIS

Born in Paris, 1911
Studied at the Sorbonne, Paris (1932–35);
École du Louvre, Paris (1936–38); École
des Beaux-Arts, Paris (1936–38);
Académie de la Grande Chaumière, Paris
(1937–38)
Lives in New York

ONE-ARTIST EXHIBITIONS

1945 Bertha Schaefer Gallery, New York
1947 Norlyst Gallery, New York
1949 Peridot Gallery, New York
1959 Andrew Dickson White Museum,
Cornell University, Ithaca, New York
1964 Stable Gallery, New York
1979 Xavier Fourcade, Inc., New York
1980 Max Hutchinson Gallery, New York
1981 Renaissance Society at the University
of Chicago
1982 Robert Miller Gallery, New York
The Museum of Modern Art, New York
(traveled)
1985 Galerie Maeght Lelong, Paris
1986 Robert Miller Gallery, New York

GROUP EXHIBITIONS

1942 The Metropolitan Museum of Art,
New York, "Artists for Victory: An
Exhibition of Painting, Sculpture and
Graphic Arts"
1944 The Museum of Modern Art,
New York, "Modern Drawings"
1945 Whitney Museum of American Art,
New York, "Annual Exhibition of
Contemporary American Painting"
1958 Whitney Museum of American Art,
New York, "Nature in Abstraction: The
Relation of Abstract Painting and
Sculpture to Nature in Twentieth-
Century American Art" (traveled)
1966 Fischbach Gallery, New York,
"Eccentric Abstraction"
1976 Whitney Museum of American Art,
New York, "200 Years of American
Sculpture"
1982 San Francisco Museum of Modern
Art, "20 American Artists: 1982
Sculpture"
1984 Hirshhorn Museum and Sculpture
Garden, Smithsonian Institution,
Washington, D.C., "Content: A
Contemporary Focus, 1974–1984"
The Museum of Modern Art, New York,
"Primitivism in 20th Century Art:
Affinity of the Tribal and Modern"
Whitney Museum of American Art, New
York, "The Third Dimension: Sculpture
of the New York School" (traveled)

BIBLIOGRAPHY

Ashton, Dore. *Modern American Sculpture.*
New York: Harry N. Abrams, 1968.
Gorovoy, Jerry. *Louise Bourgeois.* New York:
The Bellport Press, 1986.
Krauss, Rosalind E. *Passages in Modern
Sculpture.* New York: Viking Press, 1977.

Lippard, Lucy R. "Louise Bourgeois: From the Inside Out." *Artforum*, 13 (March 1975), pp. 26–33.

Pincus-Witten, Robert. *Bourgeois Truth* (exhibition catalogue). New York: Robert Miller Gallery, 1982.

Wye, Deborah. *Louise Bourgeois* (exhibition catalogue). New York: The Museum of Modern Art, 1982.

JOHN CHAMBERLAIN

Born in Rochester, Indiana, 1927
Studied at the School of the Art Institute of Chicago (1951–52); Black Mountain College, Black Mountain, North Carolina (1955–56)
Lives in New York and Sarasota, Florida

ONE-ARTIST EXHIBITIONS

1957 Wells Street Gallery, Chicago
1960 Martha Jackson Gallery, New York
1962 Leo Castelli Gallery, New York
1964 Galerie Ileana Sonnabend, Paris
1966 Dwan Gallery, Los Angeles
1971 The Solomon R. Guggenheim Museum, New York
1977 Heiner Friedrich, Inc., New York
1979 Kunsthalle Bern, Switzerland
1980 Stedelijk Van Abbemuseum, Eindhoven, The Netherlands
1983 John and Mable Ringling Museum of Art, Sarasota, Florida
1984 Xavier Fourcade, Inc., New York
1986 The Museum of Contemporary Art, Los Angeles

GROUP EXHIBITIONS

1959 The Museum of Modern Art, New York, "Recent Sculpture: USA"
1960 The Art Institute of Chicago, "65th Annual American Exhibition"
The Museum of Modern Art, New York, "The Art of Assemblage"
Whitney Museum of American Art, New York, "1960 Annual Exhibition: Contemporary Sculpture and Drawings"
1964 Venice, Italy, "XXXII Biennale di Venezia"
1969 The Metropolitan Museum of Art, New York, "New York Painting and Sculpture: 1940–1970"
1975 National Collection of Fine Arts, Smithsonian Institution, Washington, D.C., "Sculpture: American Directions 1945–75"
1976 Akademie der Künste, West Berlin, "New York—Downtown Manhattan: Soho"
Whitney Museum of American Art, New York, "200 Years of American Sculpture"
1982 Kassel, West Germany, "Documenta 7"
1985 Whitney Museum of American Art, New York, "The Third Dimension: Sculpture of the New York School" (traveled)

BIBLIOGRAPHY

Auping, Michael. *John Chamberlain Reliefs 1960–82* (exhibition catalogue). Sarasota, Florida: John and Mable Ringling Museum of Art, 1983.

Phillips, Lisa. *The Third Dimension: Sculpture of the New York School* (exhibition catalogue). New York: Whitney Museum of American Art, 1985.

Sylvester, Julie. *John Chamberlain: A Catalogue Raisonné of the Sculpture, 1954–1985*. New York: Hudson Hills Press in association with The Museum of Contemporary Art, Los Angeles, 1986.

Tuchman, Phillis. "An Interview with John Chamberlain." *Artforum*, 10 (February 1972), pp. 38–43.

Waldman, Diane. *John Chamberlain: A Retrospective Exhibition* (exhibition catalogue). New York: The Solomon R. Guggenheim Museum, 1971.

CLEGG & GUTTMANN

MICHAEL CLEGG

Born in 1957
Lives in New York

MARTIN GUTTMANN

Born in 1957
Lives in New York

TWO-ARTIST EXHIBITIONS

1981 Annina Nosei Gallery, New York
1982 Galerie Michelle Lachowsky, Antwerp
1983 Galerie Eric Fabre, Paris
Galerie Achim Kubinski, Stuttgart
1984 Cable Gallery, New York
Galerie Tanya Grunert, Cologne
1985 Cable Gallery, New York
Galerie Achim Kubinski, Stuttgart
Galerie Löhrl, Mönchengladbach, West Germany
1986 Galerie Dürr, Munich
Jay Gorney Modern Art, New York
Rotterdam Art Foundation
Galerie 'T Venster, Rotterdam

GROUP EXHIBITIONS

1984 Württembergischer Kunstverein, Stuttgart, "The Self-Portrait in Photography"
1985 Nature Morte Gallery, New York, "Infotainment" (traveled)
Galerie Philip Nelson, Lyons, "Transient Object"
1986 Galerie Bismarckstrasse, Cologne, "James Casebere, Clegg & Guttmann, Ken Lum"
Castel dell'Ovo, Naples, "Rooted Rhetoric"
Frankfurter Kunstverein und Kunsthalle, "Prospect '86"
The Queens Museum, Flushing, New York, "The Real Big Picture"

BIBLIOGRAPHY

Pelene, Arielle. *Clegg & Guttmann* (exhibition catalogue). Mönchengladbach, West Germany: Galerie Löhrl, 1985.

Welchman, John. "Clegg and Guttmann." *Flash Art*, 130 (October-November 1986), p. 70–71.

Indiana, Gary. "Signs of Empire." *The Village Voice*, December 31, 1985, p. 80.

Lawson, Thomas, David Robbins, and George W.S. Trow. *Infotainment* (exhibition catalogue). New York: Nature Morte Gallery, 1985.

GEORGE CONDO

Born in Concord, New Hampshire, 1957
Lives in Paris

ONE-ARTIST EXHIBITIONS

1983 Ulrike Kantor Gallery, Los Angeles
1984 Barbara Gladstone Gallery, New York
Pat Hearn Gallery, New York
1985 Galerie Bruno Bischofberger, Zürich
Galerie Monika Spruth, Cologne
Galerie 'T Venster, Rotterdam
1986 Barbara Gladstone Gallery, New York
Akira Ikeda Gallery, Tokyo

GROUP EXHIBITIONS

1984 Barbara Gladstone Gallery, New York, "New Hand Painted Dreams: Contemporary Surrealism"
1985 Museum Folkwang, Essen, West Germany, "Kunstliche Paradiese" (traveled)

BIBLIOGRAPHY

Collings, Matthew. "Nothing Is Important." *Artscribe*, 55 (December-January 1985–86), p. 40.

Evans-Clark, Phillip. "Neo-Surrealism, Or the Archetype of the Artist as an Ostrich." *Arts Magazine*, 60 (December 1985), pp. 26–31.

Indiana, Gary. "George Condo at Barbara Gladstone and Pat Hearn." *Art in America*, 73 (May 1985), p. 175.

———. "George Condo." *The Village Voice*, April 22, 1985, p. 99.

Pohlen, Annelie. "Kunstliche Paradiese, Museum Folkwang." *Artforum*, 24 (April 1986), pp. 121–22.

WILLEM DE KOONING

Born in Rotterdam, 1904
Studied at the Academie voor Beeldende Kunsten en Technische Wetenschappen, Rotterdam (1916–25); Académie Royale des Beaux-Arts, Brussels (1924); van Schelling Design School, Antwerp (1924)
Lives in The Springs, Long Island, New York

ONE-ARTIST EXHIBITIONS

1948 Egan Gallery, New York
1953 Sidney Janis Gallery, New York
1964 Allan Stone Gallery, New York
1967 M. Knoedler & Co., New York
1968 Stedelijk Museum, Amsterdam (traveled)
1971 The Museum of Modern Art, New York
1974 Walker Art Center, Minneapolis (traveled)
1976 Xavier Fourcade, Inc., New York
1978 The Solomon R. Guggenheim Museum, New York
1979 Museum of Art, Carnegie Institute, Pittsburgh
1983 Whitney Museum of American Art, New York (traveled)

GROUP EXHIBITIONS

1936 The Museum of Modern Art, New York, "New Horizons in American Art"
1944 Cincinnati Art Museum, "Abstract and Surrealist Art in the United States" (traveled)
1948 Whitney Museum of American Art, New York, "1948 Annual Exhibition of Contemporary American Painting"
1951 The Museum of Modern Art, New York, "Abstract Painting and Sculpture in America"
1958 Whitney Museum of American Art, New York, "Nature in Abstraction: The Relation of Abstract Painting and Sculpture to Nature in Twentieth-Century American Art" (traveled)
1959 Kassel, West Germany, "Documenta 2"
1961 The Museum of Modern Art, New York, "The Art of Assemblage" (traveled)
1970 The Metropolitan Museum of Art, New York, "New York Painting and Sculpture: 1940–1970"
Musée National d'Art Moderne, Centre Georges Pompidou, Paris, "Paris—New York"
1978 Albright-Knox Art Gallery, Buffalo, "American Painting of the 1970s" (traveled)

BIBLIOGRAPHY

Cummings, Paul, Jörn Merkert, and Claire Stoullig. Willem de Kooning: Drawings, Paintings, Sculpture (exhibition catalogue). New York: Whitney Museum of American Art in association with Prestel-Verlag, Munich, and W.W. Norton and Co., 1983.
Hess, Thomas B. Willem de Kooning. New York: George Braziller, 1959.
———. Willem de Kooning (exhibition catalogue). New York: The Museum of Modern Art, 1968.
Rosenberg, Harold. Willem de Kooning. New York: Harry N. Abrams, 1974.
Waldman, Diane. Willem de Kooning in East Hampton (exhibition catalogue). New York: The Solomon R. Guggenheim Museum, 1978.

NANCY DWYER

Born in New York, 1954
Studied at the State University of New York, College at New Paltz (1972–74); State University of New York, Empire State College, Saratoga (1975); State University of New York at Buffalo (B.F.A., 1976)
Lives in New York

ONE-ARTIST EXHIBITIONS

1980 Artists Space, New York
Hallwalls, Buffalo
1982 A&M Artworks, New York
1983 Semaphore Gallery, New York
1984 Texas Gallery, Houston
Cash/Newhouse Gallery, New York
1985 Semaphore Gallery, New York
1986 Josh Baer Gallery, New York
Cash/Newhouse Gallery, New York

GROUP EXHIBITIONS

1976 Artists Space, New York, "Hallwalls, Buffalo"
1977 Hallwalls, Buffalo, "Snow Show"
1980 The New Museum of Contemporary Art, New York, "Hallwalls: Five Years"
1982 Institute of Contemporary Art, University of Pennsylvania, Philadelphia, "Image Scavengers: Painting"
1983 São Paulo Biennial, Brazil, "The Heroic Figure" (traveled)
1985 Artists Space, New York, "A Decade of New Art"
Allen Memorial Art Museum, Oberlin College, Ohio, "After Photographs: Drawings"
1986 Metro Pictures, New York, "Group Show"

BIBLIOGRAPHY

Indiana, Gary. "Talking Back." The Village Voice, February 11, 1986, p. 84.
———. "United States." The Villiage Voice, May 20, 1986, p. 88.
Kardon, Janet. Image Scavengers: Painting (exhibition catalogue). Philadelphia: Institute of Contemporary Art, University of Pennsylvania, 1982.
Linker, Kate. "Nancy Dwyer." Artforum, 23 (May 1985), p. 99.
———. "Public Vision." Artforum, 21 (November 1982), pp. 77–78.

R.M. FISCHER

Born in New York, 1947
Studied at Long Island University, Brookville, New York (B.A., 1971); San Francisco Art Institute (M.F.A., 1973)
Lives in New York

ONE-ARTIST EXHIBITIONS

1979 Artists Space, New York
Nancy Lurie Gallery, Chicago
1981 Contemporary Arts Center, Cincinnati
Stefanotti Gallery, New York
Daniel Weinberg Gallery, San Francisco
1982 Texas Gallery, Houston
1983 Baskerville + Watson, New York
1984 Musées de la Ville de Toulon, France
Whitney Museum of American Art, New York
1985 Baskerville + Watson, New York
Daniel Weinberg Gallery, Los Angeles

GROUP EXHIBITIONS

1980 Hal Bromm Gallery, New York, "Critic's Choice"
1981 Hayden Gallery, Massachusetts Institute of Technology, Cambridge, "Body Language: Figurative Aspects of Recent Art" (traveled)
1982 Contemporary Arts Center, Cincinnati, "Dynamix" (traveled)
1983 Barbara Toll Fine Arts, New York, "Modern Objects"
Whitney Museum of American Art, New York, "1983 Biennial Exhibition"
1984 Milwaukee Art Museum, " Scott Burton, Judith Shea, R.M. Fischer: Art and Use"
Museum of Art, Rhode Island School of Design, Providence, "Furniture Furnishings: Subject and Object" (traveled)
The Museum of Modern Art, New York, "An International Survey of Recent Painting and Sculpture"
John Weber Gallery, New York, "Science Fiction"
1985 Whitney Museum of American Art, New York, "High Styles: Twentieth-Century American Design"
1986 Daniel Weinberg Gallery, Los Angeles, "Objects in the Modern World"

BIBLIOGRAPHY

Armstrong, Richard. The Sculpture of R.M. Fischer (exhibition brochure). New York: Whitney Museum of American Art, 1984.
Cameron, Dan. "The Case for R.M. Fischer." Arts Magazine, 59 (September 1984), pp. 70–73.
Domergue, Denise. Artists Design Furniture. New York: Harry N. Abrams, 1984.
Felshin, Nina. "R.M. Fischer: Lampworks." Dialogue, 3 (July-August 1981), pp. 28–30.
Smith, Roberta. Body Language: Figurative Aspects of Recent Art (exhibition catalogue). Cambridge: Hayden Gallery, Massachusetts Institute of Technology, 1982.

LOUISE FISHMAN

Born in Philadelphia, 1939
Studied at the Tyler School of Fine Arts, Philadelphia (B.S., B.F.A., 1963); University of Illinois, Urbana (M.F.A., 1965)
Lives in New York

ONE-ARTIST EXHIBITIONS

1964 Philadelphia Art Alliance
1974 Nancy Hoffman Gallery, New York
1982 Oscarsson-Hood Gallery, New York
1984 Baskerville + Watson, New York
1986 Baskerville + Watson, New York

GROUP EXHIBITIONS

1972 A.I.R. Gallery, New York, "Open A.I.R."
1973 Whitney Museum of American Art, New York, "1973 Biennial Exhibition: Contemporary American Art"
1977 Procter Art Center, Annandale-on-Hudson, New York, "Paintings That Reveal the Wall"
1982 Suzanne Lemberg Usdan Gallery, Bennington, Vermont, "Five New York Artists"
Randolph Street Gallery, Chicago, "Mixing Art and Politics"
1983 The Hudson River Museum, Yonkers, New York, "Six Artists"
1984 Cable Gallery, New York
1985 The Parrish Art Museum, Southampton, New York, "Painting as Landscape: Views of American Modernism"

BIBLIOGRAPHY

Feinberg, Jean. "Louise Fishman: New Paintings." *Arts Magazine*, 54 (November 1979), pp. 105–07.
Lancaster, Christa. "Louise Fishman." *Arts Magazine*, 56 (May 1982), p. 25.
McFadden, Sarah. "Expressionism Today: An Artists' Symposium." *Art in America*, 70 (December 1982), p. 66.
Smith, Roberta. "Louise Fishman." *The New York Times*, October 31, 1986.
Storr, Robert. "Louise Fishman at Baskerville + Watson." *Art in America*, 73 (February 1985), pp. 140–41.

ROBERT GREENE

Born in New York, 1953
Studied at Syracuse University, New York (1971–73); Pratt Institute, Brooklyn, New York (B.I.D., 1976)
Lives in New York

ONE-ARTIST EXHIBITIONS

1983 Kathleen Meyer Gallery, Louisville, Kentucky
1984 Tracey Garet Gallery, New York
1986 Robert Miller Gallery, New York
Meredith Long Gallery, Houston

GROUP EXHIBITIONS

1981 Harriman College Art Gallery, Harriman, New York, "CAPS Exhibition"
The Hudson River Museum, Yonkers, New York, "People '81"
1985 Dog Museum of America, New York, "Era of the Pet: Four Centuries of People and Their Dogs"
Galeria Leyendeker, Santa Cruz de Tenerife, Canary Islands, "Group Show"
1986 CDS Gallery, New York, "13 Americans"
Robert Miller Gallery, New York, "Gallery Group Show"

BIBLIOGRAPHY

Henry, Gerrit. "Robert Greene at Robert Miller." *Art in America*, 74 (May 1986), p. 161.
Mathews, Margaret O. "A Young Artist Faces the Challenge of Success." *American Artist*, 50 (June 1986), pp. 76–79.
Slaton, Amy. "Robert Greene at Tracey Garet." *East Village Eye*, December-January 1984–85.

PETER HALLEY

Born in New York, 1953
Studied at Yale University, New Haven (B.A., 1975); University of New Orleans (M.F.A., 1978)
Lives in New York

ONE-ARTIST EXHIBITIONS

1978 Contemporary Arts Center, New Orleans
1980 P.S. 122 Gallery, New York
1985 International With Monument Gallery, New York
1986 Daniel Templon Gallery, Paris
International With Monument Gallery, New York

GROUP EXHIBITIONS

1984 White Columns, New York, "The New Capital"
Baskerville + Watson, New York, "Brilliant Color"
1985 Institute of Contemporary Art, Boston, "Currents"
Metro Pictures, New York, "Selected Work"
Postmasters Gallery, New York, "Paravision"
1986 Cleveland Center for Contemporary Art, "New New York"
La Fundació Caixa de Pensions, Barcelona, "L'Art i el Seu Doble. Panorama de l'Art a Nova York"
Institute of Contemporary Art, Boston, "End Game: Reference and Simulation in Recent Painting and Sculpture"
Sonnabend Gallery, New York, "Group Show"

BIBLIOGRAPHY

Berger, Maurice. *Political Geometries: On the Meaning of Alienation* (exhibition catalogue). New York: Hunter College Art Gallery, 1986.
Cameron, Dan. *L'Art i el Seu Doble. Panorama de l'Art a Nova York* (exhibition catalogue). Barcelona: La Fundació Caixa de Pensions, 1986.
Collins, Tricia, and Richard Milazzo. "Tropical Codes." *Kunstforum International*, March, April, May 1986, pp. 308–37.
Madoff, Steven. "Vestiges and Ruins: Ethics and Geometric Art in the Twentieth Century." *Arts Magazine*, 61 (December 1986), pp. 32–40.
Russell, John. "Bright Young Talents: Six Artists with a Future." *The New York Times*, May 18, 1986, section II, p. 1.

ROBERT HELM

Born in Wallace, Idaho, 1943
Studied at Washington State University, Pullman (B.A., 1967; M.F.A., 1969)
Lives in Pullman, Washington

ONE-ARTIST EXHIBITIONS

1974 Museum of Art, Washington State University, Pullman
1976 Nicholas Wilder Gallery, Los Angeles
1977 Faith and Charity in Hope Gallery, Hope, Idaho
1982 Galerie Redmann, West Berlin
1984 Contemporary Arts Museum, Houston
L.A. Louver Gallery, Venice, California
Seattle Art Museum

GROUP EXHIBITIONS

1969 Cheney Cowles Memorial Museum, Spokane, Washington, "Northwest Annual"
1975 Missoula Museum of the Arts, Missoula, Montana, "Concepts and Executions of 8 Sculptors"
Museum of Art, Washington State University, Pullman, "Northwest Sculpture"
Musée d'Art Moderne de la Ville de Paris, "10me Biennale de Paris"
1985 Crocker Art Museum, Sacramento, California, "Contemporary American Wood Sculpture"
1986 Neuberger Museum, State University of New York at Purchase, "Awards in the Visual Arts 5" (traveled)

BIBLIOGRAPHY

Gambrell, Jamey. *Awards in the Visual Arts 5* (exhibition catalogue). Winston-Salem, North Carolina: The Southeastern Center for Contemporary Art, 1986.
Glowen, Ron. "Robert Helm at Seattle Art Museum." *Art in America*, 72 (May 1984), p. 181.
Guenther, Bruce. *50 Northwest Artists*. San Francisco: Chronicle Books, 1983.
Ivory, James. "In the American Grain: Robert Helm." *Artforum*, 23 (November 1984), pp. 74–76.

NEIL JENNEY

Born in Torrington, Connecticut, 1945
Studied at the Massachusetts College of
   Art, Boston (1964–66)
Lives in New York

ONE-ARTIST EXHIBITIONS

1968 Galerie Rudolf Zwirner, Cologne
1970 Richard Bellamy/Noah Goldowsky
   Gallery, New York
   David Whitney Gallery, New York
1974 Blum Helman Gallery, New York
1975 Wadsworth Atheneum, Hartford,
   Connecticut
1981 University Art Museum, University of
   California, Berkeley (traveled)
1984 Oil and Steel Gallery, New York
1985 Carpenter + Hochman Gallery,
   New York

GROUP EXHIBITIONS

1967 Richard Bellamy/Noah Goldowsky
   Gallery, New York, "Arp to
   Artschwager: 2nd Annual Exhibition"
1969 Andrew Dickson White Museum,
   Cornell University, Ithaca, New York,
   "Earth Art"
   Kunsthalle Bern, Switzerland, "Live in
   Your Head: When Attitudes Become
   Form (Works—Concepts—Processes—
   Situations—Information)" (traveled)
   Whitney Museum of American Art, New
   York, "Anti-Illusion: Procedures/
   Materials"
1972 Kassel, West Germany, "Documenta 5"
1976 New York State Museum, Albany,
   "New York: The State of Art"
1978 The New Museum of Contemporary
   Art, New York, "'Bad' Painting"
   Whitney Museum of American Art,
   New York, "New Image Painting"
1984 Whitney Museum of American Art,
   New York, "American Art Since 1970:
   Painting, Sculpture, and Drawings from
   the Collection of the Whitney Museum
   of American Art" (traveled)
1986 The Art Institute of Chicago,
   "Seventy-fifth American Exhibition"

BIBLIOGRAPHY

Marshall, Richard. *New Image Painting*
   (exhibition catalogue). New York:
   Whitney Museum of American Art, 1978.
Rosenthal, Mark. *Neil Jenney: Paintings and
   Sculpture, 1967–1980* (exhibition
   catalogue). Berkeley: University Art
   Museum, University of California, 1981.
Tucker, Marcia. *"Bad" Painting* (exhibition
   catalogue). New York: The New Museum
   of Contemporary Art, 1978.
————, and James Monte. *Anti-Illusion:
   Procedures/Materials* (exhibition
   catalogue). New York: Whitney Museum
   of American Art, 1969.

ROBERTO JUAREZ

Born in Chicago, 1952
Studied at the San Francisco Art Institute
   (B.F.A., 1977); University of California,
   Los Angeles (1978–79)
Lives in New York

ONE-ARTIST EXHIBITIONS

1977 San Francisco Art Institute
1981 Robert Miller Gallery, New York
1983 Mira Godard Gallery, Toronto
   Robert Miller Gallery, New York
1984 André Emmerich Gallery, Zurich
   Robert Miller Gallery, New York
   Betsy Rosenfield Gallery, Chicago
1985 La Mama-La Galleria Second Classe,
   New York
   Texas Gallery, Houston
1986 Galeria Juana de Aizpuru, Madrid
   Robert Miller Gallery, New York

GROUP EXHIBITIONS

1981 The Aldrich Museum of
   Contemporary Art, Ridgefield,
   Connecticut, "New Visions"
   P.S. 1, Institute for Art and Urban
   Resources, New York, "New Wave, New
   York" (traveled)
1982 Museum of Art, Fort Lauderdale,
   "New Directions: Contemporary
   American Art from the Commodities
   Corporation Collection" (traveled)
   Sidney Janis Gallery, New York, "The
   Expressionist Image: American Art from
   Pollock to Today"
1983 The Brooklyn Museum, New York,
   "The American Artist as Printmaker"
   Rheinisches Landesmuseum Bonn, "Back
   to the USA: Amerikanische Kunst der
   Siebziger und Achtziger (traveled)
1984 The Museum of Modern Art, New
   York, "An International Survey of Recent
   Painting and Sculpture"
   Indianapolis Museum of Art, "Painting
   and Sculpture Today"
1985 Weatherspoon Art Gallery, University
   of North Carolina at Greensboro, "Art
   on Paper 1985"

BIBLIOGRAPHY

Castle, Frederick Ted. "Roberto Juarez at
   Robert Miller." *Art in America*, 73 (March
   1985), p. 152.
Glueck, Grace, "Roberto Juarez, Robert
   Miller Gallery." *The New York Times*,
   January 28, 1983, p. C19.
Honnef, Klaus, ed. *Back to the USA:
   Amerikanische Kunst der Siebziger und
   Achtziger* (exhibition catalogue). Bonn:
   Rheinisches Landesmuseum Bonn, 1983.
Indiana, Gary. *Roberto Juarez* (exhibition
   catalogue). New York: Robert Miller
   Gallery, 1986.
McShine, Kynaston. *An International Survey
   of Recent Painting and Sculpture* (exhibition
   catalogue). New York: The Museum of
   Modern Art, 1984.

JEFF KOONS

Born in York, Pennsylvania, 1955
Studied at the Maryland Institute College
   of Art, Baltimore (1972–75); School of
   the Art Institute of Chicago (1975–76);
   Maryland Institute College of Art,
   Baltimore (B.F.A., 1976)
Lives in New York

ONE-ARTIST EXHIBITIONS

1980 The New Museum of Contemporary
   Art, New York
1985 Feature Gallery, Chicago
   International With Monument Gallery,
   New York
1986 International With Monument
   Gallery, New York
   Daniel Weinberg Gallery, Los Angeles

GROUP EXHIBITIONS

1981 P.S. 1, Institute for Art and Urban
   Resources, Long Island City, New York,
   "Lighting"
1982 Artists Space, New York, "A Likely
   Story"
   Renaissance Society at the University of
   Chicago, "A Fatal Attraction: Art and the
   Media"
1985 The Kitchen, New York, "Objects in
   Collision"
   Postmasters Gallery, New York,
   "Paravision"
   Whitney Museum of American Art,
   Fairfield County, Stamford, Connecticut,
   "Affiliations: Recent Sculpture and Its
   Antecedents"
1986 La Fundació Caixa de Pensions,
   Barcelona, "L'Art i el Seu Doble.
   Panorama de l'Art a Nova York"
   Institute of Contemporary Art, Boston,
   "End Game: Reference and Simulation in
   Recent Painting and Sculpture"
   The New Museum of Contemporary Art,
   New York, "Damaged Goods: Desire
   and the Economy of the Object"
   Sonnabend Gallery, New York,
   "Group Show"

BIBLIOGRAPHY

Cameron, Dan. "Pretty as a Product." *Arts
   Magazine*, 60 (May 1986), p. 22.
Collins, Tricia, and Richard Milazzo.
   "Tropical Codes." *Kunstforum
   International*, March, April, May 1986, pp.
   308–37.
Indiana, Gary. "Jeff Koons at International
   With Monument." *Art in America*, 73
   (November 1985), pp. 163–64.
Lawson, Thomas. *A Fatal Attraction: Art and
   the Media* (exhibition catalogue).
   Chicago: Renaissance Society at the
   University of Chicago, 1982.
Wallis, Brian, ed. *Damaged Goods: Desire and
   the Economy of the Object* (exhibition
   catalogue). New York: The New Museum
   of Contemporary Art, 1986.

JOSEPH KOSUTH

Born in Toledo, Ohio, 1945
Studied at the Cleveland Institute of Art
(1963–64); School of Visual Arts, New
York (1966–67)
Lives in New York

ONE-ARTIST EXHIBITIONS

1969 Kunsthalle Bern, Switzerland
Leo Castelli Gallery, New York
1970 Pasadena Art Museum, California
1971 Galerie Paul Maenz, Cologne
Galerie Bruno Bischofberger, Zurich
1976 Renaissance Society at the University
of Chicago
1978 Museum of Modern Art, Oxford
Stedelijk Van Abbemuseum, Eindhoven,
The Netherlands
1980 P.S. 1, Institute for Art and Urban
Resources, Long Island City, New York
1981 Staatsgalerie Stuttgart
1985 Musée Saint Pierre Art
Contemporain, Lyons
1986 Leo Castelli Gallery, New York

GROUP EXHIBITIONS

1974 The Art Institute of Chicago, "Idea
and Image in Recent Art"
1977 Akademie der Künste, West Berlin,
"New York—Downtown Manhattan:
Soho" (traveled)
Australian National Gallery, Canberra,
"Illusion and Reality" (traveled)
The Solomon R. Guggenheim Museum,
New York, "American Postwar Painting
from the Guggenheim Collection"
1979 Museum of Contemporary Art,
Chicago, "Concept/Narrative/Document:
Recent Photographic Works from the
Morton Neumann Family Collection"
1980 The Museum of Modern Art, New
York, "Printed Art: A View of Two
Decades"
1982 Stedelijk Museum, Amsterdam, "'60–
'80: Attitudes/Concepts/Images"
Kassel, West Germany, "Documenta 7"
1984 Hirshhorn Museum and Sculpture
Garden, Smithsonian Institution,
Washington, D.C., "Content: A
Contemporary Focus, 1974–1984"
1985 Museum of Art, Fort Lauderdale,
"An American Renaissance: Painting and
Sculpture Since 1940"
1986 Castel dell'Ovo, Naples, "Rooted
Rhetoric"

BIBLIOGRAPHY

Baker, Elizabeth C. "Joseph Kosuth:
Information, Please." *Art News*, 72
(February 1973), pp. 30–31.
Guerico, Gabriele. *Rooted Rhetoric*
(exhibition catalogue). Naples: Castel
dell'Ovo, 1986.
Indiana, Gary. "Canceled Texts." *The
Village Voice*, June 10, 1986, p. 77.
Kosuth, Joseph. "Art after Philosophy."
Studio International, 178 (October 1969),
pp. 134–37.
———. "Art after Philosophy, Part II,
'Conceptual Art' and Recent Art." *Studio
International*, 178 (November 1969),
pp. 160–61.
———. "Art after Philosophy, Part 3."
Studio International, 178 (December 1969),
pp. 212–13.

BARBARA KRUGER

Born in Newark, New Jersey, 1945
Studied at Syracuse University, New York
(1967–68); Parsons School of Design,
New York (1968–69); School of Visual
Arts, New York (1968–69)
Lives in New York

ONE-ARTIST EXHIBITIONS

1974 Artists Space, New York
1979 Franklin Furnace, New York
Printed Matter, New York
1980 P.S. 1, Institute for Art and Urban
Resources, Long Island City, New York
1982 Larry Gagosian Gallery, Los Angeles
1984 Rhona Hoffman Gallery, Chicago
Kunsthalle Basel, Switzerland
Annina Nosei Gallery, New York
1985 Contemporary Arts Museum,
Houston
Los Angeles County Museum of Art
Wadsworth Atheneum, Hartford,
Connecticut
1986 Annina Nosei Gallery, New York

GROUP EXHIBITIONS

1973 Whitney Museum of American Art,
New York, "1973 Biennial Exhibition:
Contemporary American Art"
1982 Institute of Contemporary Art,
University of Pennsylvania, Philadelphia,
"Image Scavengers: Photography"
Kassel, West Germany, "Documenta 7"
Venice, Italy, "XL Biennale di Venezia"
1984 The New Museum of Contemporary
Art, New York, "Difference: On
Representation and Sexuality" (traveled)
1985 Whitney Museum of American Art,
New York "1985 Biennial Exhibition"
1986 The Corcoran Gallery of Art,
Washington, D.C., "Spectrum: In Other
Words"
La Fundació Caixa de Pensions,
Barcelona, "L'Art i el Seu Doble.
Panorama de l'Art a Nova York"
Institute of Contemporary Art, Boston,
"Dissent: The Issue of Modern Art in
Boston"
The Queens Museum, Flushing, New
York, "The Real Big Picture"

BIBLIOGRAPHY

Buchloh, Benjamin H.D. "Allegorical
Procedures: Appropriation and Montage
in Contemporary Art." *Artforum*, 21
(September 1982), pp. 43–56.
Grundberg, Andy. "Pictures That Poke Fun
at Power." *The New York Times*, April 1,
1984, p. H31.
Linker, Kate. "Barbara Kruger." *Flash Art*,
121 (March 1985), pp. 36–37.
Owens, Craig. "The Medusa Effect, or the
Specular Ruse." *Art in America*, 72
(January 1984), pp. 97–105.
———, and Jane Weinstock. *We Won't Play
Nature to Your Culture* (exhibition
catalogue). London: Institute of
Contemporary Arts, 1983.

ANNETTE LEMIEUX

Born in Norfolk, Virginia, 1957
Studied at Hartford Art School, University
of Hartford, West Hartford, Connecticut
(B.F.A., 1980)
Lives in New York

ONE-ARTIST EXHIBITIONS

1980 Joseloff Gallery, Hartford Art School,
University of Hartford, West Hartford,
Connecticut
1984 Cash/Newhouse Gallery, New York
1986 Cash/Newhouse Gallery, New York

GROUP EXHIBITIONS

1985 Charlottenborg Exhibition Hall,
Copenhagen, "A Brave New World:
A New Generation"
Cash/Newhouse Gallery, New York,
"Thought Objects"
Holly Solomon Gallery, New York,
"57 St. Between A & D"

BIBLIOGRAPHY

Brooks, Rosetta. "Remembrance of Objects
Past." *Artforum*, 25 (December 1986),
pp. 68–69.
Cameron, Dan. "Report from the Front."
Arts Magazine, 60 (Summer 1986),
pp. 86–93.
Indiana, Gary. "Formal Wares." *The Village
Voice*, March 25, 1986, p. 85.
Linker, Kate. "Eluding Definition."
Artforum, 23 (December 1984), pp. 61–67.
Solomon, Thomas. *A Brave New World: A
New Generation* (exhibition catalogue).
Copenhagen: Charlottenborg Exhibition
Hall, 1985.

SOL LeWITT

Born in Hartford, Connecticut, 1928
Studied at Syracuse University, New York
(B.F.A., 1949)
Lives in Chester, Connecticut

ONE-ARTIST EXHIBITIONS

1966 Dwan Gallery, New York
1969 Museum Haus Lange, Krefeld,
West Germany

1971 John Weber Gallery, New York
1973 Galerie Yvon Lambert, Paris
1977 John Weber Gallery, New York
1978 The Museum of Modern Art, New York (traveled)
1982 Barbara Toll Fine Arts, New York
John Weber Gallery, New York
1985 Haags Gemeentemuseum, The Haag, The Netherlands
1986 John Weber Gallery, New York

GROUP EXHIBITIONS

1966 Finch College Museum of Art, New York, "Art in Progress"
The Jewish Museum, New York, "Primary Structures"
1968 Kassel, West Germany, "Documenta 4"
The Museum of Modern Art, New York, "The Art of the Real: USA 1948–1968" (traveled)
1969 Museum of Contemporary Art, Chicago, "Art by Telephone"
1972 Institute of Contemporary Art, University of Pennsylvania, Philadelphia, "Grids"
1976 Whitney Museum of American Art, New York, "200 Years of American Sculpture"
1983 The Museum of Contemporary Art, Los Angeles, "The First Show: Painting and Sculpture from Eight Collections, 1940–1980"
1984 Whitney Museum of American Art, New York, "American Art Since 1970: Painting, Sculpture, and Drawings from the Collection of the Whitney Museum of American Art, New York" (traveled)
1985 Musée d'Art Contemporain de Bordeaux, France, "Art Minimal I: Carl Andre, Donald Judd, Sol LeWitt, Robert Mangold, Robert Morris"
Museum of Art, Carnegie Institute, Pittsburgh, "1985 Carnegie International"

BIBLIOGRAPHY

Armstrong, Richard. "Sol LeWitt." *Artforum*, 21 (March 1983) pp. 70–71.
Legg, Alicia, ed. *Sol LeWitt* (exhibition catalogue). New York: The Museum of Modern Art, 1978.
Pincus-Witten, Robert. "Sol LeWitt: Word Object." *Artforum*, 11 (February 1973), pp. 69–72.
Singer, Susanna, ed. *Sol LeWitt Wall Drawings* (exhibition catalogue). Eindhoven, The Netherlands: Stedelijk Van Abbemuseum, 1984.

ROBERT LOBE

Born in Detroit, 1945
Studied at Oberlin College, Ohio (B.A., 1967); Hunter College, New York (1967–68)
Lives in New York

ONE-ARTIST EXHIBITIONS

1974 Zabriskie Gallery, New York
1977 Dag Hammerskjold Plaza Sculpture Garden, New York
1980 Willard Gallery, New York
1981 Willard Gallery, New York
1982 Texas Gallery, Houston
1984 Willard Gallery, New York
1986 Marian Locks Gallery, Philadelphia
Willard Gallery, New York

GROUP EXHIBITIONS

1969 The Detroit Institute of Arts, "Other Ideas"
Whitney Museum of American Art, New York, "Anti-Illusion: Procedures/Materials"
1973 Whitney Museum of American Art, New York, "1973 Biennial Exhibition: Contemporary American Art"
1976 P.S. 1, Institute for Art and Urban Resources, Long Island City, New York, "A Month of Sundays"
1978 The Solomon R. Guggenheim Museum, New York, "Young American Artists: 1978 Exxon National Exhibition"
1979 Albright-Knox Art Gallery, Buffalo, "Eight Sculptors"
1981 Contemporary Arts Museum, Houston, "The Americans: The Landscape"
1983 High Museum, Atlanta, "Directions in Abstraction: The Uses of Nature"
1985 Margo Leavin Gallery, Los Angeles, "Louisa Chase: Painting—Robert Lobe: Sculpture"
1986 P.S. 1, Institute for Art and Urban Resources, Long Island City, New York, "About Contemporary American Landscape"

BIBLIOGRAPHY

Armstrong, Richard. "Robert Lobe." *Artforum*, 22 (May 1984), pp. 87–88.
Baker, Kenneth. "Robert Lobe at Willard." *Art in America*, 72 (May 1984), pp. 177–78.
Cathcart, Linda L. *The Americans: The Landscape* (exhibition catalogue). Houston: Contemporary Arts Museum, 1981.
Morrin, Peter. *Directions in Abstraction: The Uses of Nature* (exhibition catalogue). Atlanta: High Museum, 1983.
Tuchman, Phyllis. "Robert Lobe at Willard." *Art in America*, 68 (September 1980), pp. 123–24.

JIM LUTES

Born in Fort Lewis, Washington, 1955
Studied at Washington State University, Pullman (B.A., 1978); School of the Art Institute of Chicago (M.F.A., 1982)
Lives in Chicago

ONE-ARTIST EXHIBITIONS

1985 Walker Art Center, Minneapolis
1986 Dart Gallery, Chicago

GROUP EXHIBITIONS

1983 Hyde Park Art Center, Chicago, "Fantastic Visions"
Renaissance Society at the University of Chicago, "Emerging"
Randolph Street Gallery, Chicago, "Jim Lutes/Jin Soo Kim"
1984 The Art Institute of Chicago, "Chicago and Vicinity"
Dart Gallery, Chicago, "Chicago 1984: Artists to Watch"
Hal Bromm Gallery, New York, "New Talent"
1985 The Corcoran Gallery of Art, Washington, D.C., "The 39th Biennial Exhibition of Contemporary American Painting"
Dart Gallery, Chicago, "A Chicago Souvenir"
1986 Artists Space, New York, "Recent Art from Chicago"

BIBLIOGRAPHY

Bonesteel, Michael. "Report from the Midwest: The 39th Corcoran Biennial: The Death Knell of Regionalism?" *Art in America*, 73 (October 1985), pp. 31–37.
Elsasser, Glen. "D.C. Exhibit Mines Art of Midwest to Spotlight a Talented American Region." *Chicago Tribune*, February 24, 1985, pp. 24–25.
Lyons, Lisa. *The 39th Biennial Exhibition of Contemporary American Painting* (exhibition catalogue). Washington, D.C.: The Corcoran Gallery of Art.
Riddle, Mason. "Doug Argue/Jim Lutes." *New Art Examiner*, 13 (April 1986), p. 65.

DAVID McDERMOTT AND PETER McGOUGH

DAVID McDERMOTT

Born in Hollywood, 1952
Studied at Syracuse University, New York (1970–74)
Lives in New York

PETER McGOUGH

Born in Syracuse, New York, 1958
Studied at Syracuse University, New York (1976); Fashion Institute of Technology, New York (1977)
Lives in New York

TWO-ARTIST EXHIBITIONS

1985 Massimo Audiello Gallery, New York
1986 Lucio Amelio, Naples
Massimo Audiello Gallery, New York
Frankfurter Kunstverein
Pat Hearn Gallery, New York

GROUP EXHIBITIONS

1983 Monique Knowlton Gallery, New York, "Intoxication"
1984 Patrick Fox Gallery, New York, "Group Show"
Holly Solomon Gallery, New York, "Group Show"
1985 Massimo Audiello Gallery, New York, "The Chi-Chi Show"
Galerie Rudolf Zwirner, Cologne, "Group Show"
1986 Mario Diacono Gallery, Boston, "Group Show"
Hallwalls, Buffalo, "Poetic Mediations"
Tony Shafrazi Gallery, New York, "What It Is"

BIBLIOGRAPHY

Black, Carl John, and Diego Cortez. *Fine Art Pictorial Guide of the Hudson River Valley* (exhibition catalogue). Naples: Lucio Amelio, 1986.
Cortez, Diego. "AIDS: The Advent of the Infinite Divine Spirit." *Flash Art*, 129 (Summer 1986), pp. 58–61.
deAk, Edit. *Some Modern Artists and Their Work* (exhibition catalogue). New York: Massimo Audiello Gallery and Pat Hearn Gallery, 1986.
Dickhoff, Wilfried, ed. *What It Is* (exhibition catalogue). New York: Tony Shafrazi Gallery, 1986.
Ratcliff, Carter. "Modern Life." *Artforum*, 24 (May 1986), p. 12.

STEPHEN MUELLER

Born in Norfolk, Virginia, 1947
Studied at the University of Texas at Austin (B.F.A., 1969); Bennington College, Bennington, Vermont (M.F.A., 1971)
Lives in New York

ONE-ARTIST EXHIBITIONS

1970 Richard L. Feigen & Co., New York
1971 Bennington College Art Gallery, Bennington, Vermont
Tibor de Nagy Gallery, New York
1972 Texas Gallery, Houston
1975 Tibor de Nagy Gallery, New York
1980 Mary Boone Gallery, New York
1982 Annina Nosei Galley, New York
1984 Annina Nosei Gallery, New York
1985 Fabian Carlsson Gallery, London
1986 Annina Nosei Gallery, New York

GROUP EXHIBITIONS

1971 Contemporary Arts Center, Cincinnati, "Young American Artists"
1973 Harcus Krakow Gallery, Boston, "Group Show"
1980 P.S. 1, Institute for Art and Urban Resources, Long Island City, New York, "Watercolors"
1981 Delahunty Gallery, Dallas, "Committed to Paint"

1982 Hamilton Gallery, New York, "The Abstract Image"
Hayden Gallery, Massachusetts Institute of Technology, Cambridge, "Two Painters on Paper"
1984 Cable Gallery, New York, "Group Show"
1984 The Parrish Art Museum, Southampton, New York, "Painting as Landscape: Views of American Modernism" (traveled)
1986 P.S. 1, Institute for Art and Urban Resources, Long Island City, New York, "About Place: Contemporary American Landscape"

BIBLIOGRAPHY

Adams, Brooks. "Stephen Mueller at Annina Nosei." *Art in America*, 70 (December 1982), pp. 123–24.
Kertess, Klaus. *Painting as Landscape: Views of American Modernism* (exhibition catalogue). Southampton, New York: The Parrish Art Museum, 1984.
———. "Painting Metaphorically: The Recent Work of Gary Stephan, Stephen Mueller, and Bill Jensen." *Artforum*, 20 (October 1981), pp. 54–58.
Ratcliff, Carter. "Painterly Versus Painted." *Art News Annual*, 37 (1970), pp. 129–47.
Yau, John. *Stephen Mueller* (exhibition catalogue). London: Fabian Carlsson Gallery, 1985.

BRUCE NAUMAN

Born in Fort Wayne, Indiana, 1941
Studied at the University of Wisconsin, Madison (B.S., 1964); University of California, Davis (M.A., 1966)
Lives in Pecos, New Mexico

ONE-ARTIST EXHIBITIONS

1966 Nicholas Wilder Gallery, Los Angeles
1968 Leo Castelli Gallery, New York
1969 Galerie Ileana Sonnabend, Paris
1971 Helman Gallery, St. Louis
1972 Los Angeles County Museum of Art (traveled)
1975 Albright-Knox Art Gallery, Buffalo
1979 Portland Center for the Visual Arts, Oregon
1981 Rijksmuseum Kröller-Müller, Otterlo, The Netherlands (traveled)
1982 The Baltimore Museum of Art
1984 Leo Castelli Gallery, New York
1986 Whitechapel Art Gallery, London (traveled)

GROUP EXHIBITIONS

1967 Los Angeles County Museum of Art, "American Sculpture of the Sixties" (traveled)
1969 Kunsthalle Bern, Switzerland, "Live in Your Head: When Attitudes Become Form (Works—Concepts—Processes—Situations—Information)" (traveled)

Whitney Museum of American Art, New York, "Anti-Illusion: Procedures/Materials"
1970 The Museum of Modern Art, New York, "Information"
1975 Museum of Contemporary Art, Chicago, "Bodyworks"
1976 San Francisco Museum of Modern Art, "Painting and Sculpture in California: The Modern Era" (traveled)
1979 Museum Bochum, West Germany, "Words Words" (traveled)
1981 Los Angeles County Museum of Art, "Art in Los Angeles—Seventeen Artists in the Sixties"
1982 Stedelijk Museum, Amsterdam, "'60–'80: Attitudes/Concepts/Images"
1985 The Museum of Modern Art, New York, "New Work on Paper 3"

BIBLIOGRAPHY

Livingston, Jane, and Marcia Tucker. *Bruce Nauman: Work from 1965 to 1972* (exhibition catalogue). Los Angeles: Los Angeles County Museum of Art and the Whitney Museum of American Art, New York, 1972.
Pincus-Witten, Robert. "New York: Bruce Nauman." *Artforum*, 6 (April 1968), pp. 63–64.
———. "Bruce Nauman: Another Kind of Reasoning." *Artforum*, 10 (February 1972), pp. 30–37.
Richardson, Brenda. *Bruce Nauman: Neons* (exhibition catalogue). Baltimore: The Baltimore Museum of Art, 1982.
Serota, Nicholas, ed. *Bruce Nauman* (exhibition catalogue). London: Whitechapel Art Gallery, 1986. Essays by Joan Simon and Jean-Christophe Ammann.

NAM JUNE PAIK

Born in Seoul, Korea, 1932
Studied at the University of Tokyo (B.A., 1956)
Lives in New York

ONE-ARTIST EXHIBITIONS

1963 Galerie Parnass, Wuppertal, West Germany
1965 New School for Social Research, New York
1968 Galeria Bonino, New York
1974 Everson Museum of Art of Syracuse and Onondaga County, Syracuse, New York
1975 René Block Gallery, New York
1976 Kölnischer Kunstverein, Cologne
1977 The Museum of Modern Art, New York
1982 Whitney Museum of American Art, New York (traveled)
Museum of Contemporary Art, Chicago
1986 Holly Solomon Gallery, New York

GROUP EXHIBITIONS

1966 Institute of Contemporary Art,
Boston, "Art Turns On"
1967 Howard Wise Gallery, New York,
"Festival of Light"
Walker Art Center, Minneapolis, "Light,
Motion, Space"
1968 The Museum of Modern Art, New
York, "The Machine as Seen at the End
of the Mechanical Age"
1969 Howard Wise Gallery, New York,
"TV as a Creative Medium"
1970 Rose Art Museum, Brandeis
University, Waltham, Massachusetts
"Vision and Television"
1971 Whitney Museum of American Art,
New York, "Videoshow"
1977 Kassel, West Germany, "Documenta 6"
1979 Museum Moderner Kunst, Vienna,
"Sammlung Hahn"
1981 Whitney Museum of American Art,
New York, "1981 Biennial Exhibition"

BIBLIOGRAPHY

Hanhardt, John G., ed. *Nam June Paik*
(exhibition catalogue). New York:
Whitney Museum of American Art, 1982.
Essays by John G. Hanhardt, Michael
Nyman, Dieter Ronte, and David A.
Ross.
Herzogenrath, Wulf. *Nam June Paik: Fluxus,
Video*. Munich: Verlag Silke Schreiber,
1983.
Paik, Nam June. *Art for 25 Million People:
Bonjour Monsieur Orwell: Kunst und
Satelliten in der Zukunft*. West Berlin:
Daadgalerie, 1984.
Rosebush, Judson. *Nam June Paik: Videa 'n'
Videology, 1959–1973*. Syracuse, New
York: Everson Museum of Art of
Syracuse and Onondaga County, 1974.
Tokyo Metropolitan Museum in
collaboration with the Japanese
Foundation. *Nam June Paik: Mostly Video*
(exhibition catalogue). Tokyo, 1984.

IZHAR PATKIN

Born in Haifa, Israel, 1955
Studied at the Corcoran Gallery School of
Art, Washington, D.C. (B.F.A., 1979);
Independent Study Program, Whitney
Museum of American Art, New York,
(1979–80)
Lives in New York

ONE-ARTIST EXHIBITIONS

1981 The Kitchen, New York
1983 Holly Solomon Gallery, New York
1984 Holly Solomon Gallery, New York
1985 Holly Solomon Gallery, New York
1986 Artspace, San Francisco
Limbo Gallery, New York

GROUP EXHIBITIONS

1981 C. Space, New York, "PhPhoto"
1982 Daniel Wolf Gallery, New York,
"Photographs By/Photographs In"
The Chrysler Museum, Norfolk, Virginia,
"Still Modern after All These Years"
1983 Monique Knowlton Gallery, New
York, "Intoxication"
Rheinisches Landesmuseum Bonn, "Back
to the USA: Amerikanische Kunst der
Siebziger und Achtziger" (traveled)
1984 Indianapolis Museum of Art,
"Painting and Sculpture Today: 1984"
P.S. 1, Institute for Art and Urban
Resources, Long Island City, New York,
"The Portrait Show"
1985 Wessel-O'Conner Gallery, Rome,
"Discovery of America"

BIBLIOGRAPHY

Cameron, Dan. "Izhar Patkin." *Flash Art*,
129 (Summer 1986), pp. 70–71.
Indiana, Gary. "Imitation of Life." *The
Village Voice*, April 29, 1986, p. 88.
Patkin, Izhar. "Who Changes the Lock? A
Conversation with Herbert Muschamp."
New Observations, 35 (1985), pp. 11–14.
Ricard, René. "The Radiant Child."
Artforum, 20 (December 1981),
pp. 35–43.
Taylor, Paul. "Izhar Patkin: Behind the
Rubber Curtain." *The Face*, April 25,
1986, p. 21.

JUDY PFAFF

Born in London, 1946
Studied at Wayne State University, Detroit
(1965–66); Southern Illinois University,
Edwardsville (1968–69); Washington
University, St. Louis (B.F.A., 1971); Yale
University Summer School of Music and
Art, Norfolk, Connecticut (1970); Yale
University, New Haven (M.F.A., 1973)
Lives in New York

ONE-ARTIST EXHIBITIONS

1974 Webb and Parsons Gallery, Bedford,
New York
1975 Artists Space, New York
1980 Holly Solomon Gallery, New York
1981 John and Mable Ringling Museum of
Art, Sarasota, Florida
1982 Albright-Knox Art Gallery, Buffalo
Bennington College Art Gallery,
Bennington, Vermont
University Gallery, University of
Massachusetts, Amherst
1985 Wacoal Art Center, Tokyo
1986 Knight Gallery/Spririt Square Arts
Center, Charlotte, North Carolina
Holly Solomon Gallery, New York

GROUP EXHIBITIONS

1975 Whitney Museum of American Art,
New York, "1975 Biennial Exhibition"

1979 Neuberger Museum, State University
of New York at Purchase, "Ten Artists/
Artists Space"
1980 Contemporary Arts Museum,
Houston, "Extensions: Jennifer Bartlett,
Lynda Benglis, Robert Longo, Judy
Pfaff"
1981 Whitney Museum of American Art,
New York, "1981 Biennial Exhibition"
Hirshhorn Museum and Sculpture
Garden, Smithsonian Institution,
Washington, D.C., "Directions 1981"
Hayden Gallery, Massachusetts Institute
of Technology, Cambridge, "Body
Language: Figurative Aspects of
Recent Art"
1983 Rheinisches Landesmuseum Bonn,
"Back to the USA: Amerikanische Kunst
der Siebziger und Achtziger" (traveled)
The Tate Gallery, London, "New Art"
1984 The Museum of Modern Art, New
York, "An International Survey of Recent
Painting and Sculpture"
Venice, Italy, "XLI Biennale di Venezia
1985 The Brooklyn Museum, New York,
"Working in Brooklyn: Sculpture"

BIBLIOGRAPHY

Armstrong, Richard. "Judy Pfaff." *Los
Angeles Institute of Contemporary Art
Journal*, 19 (June-July 1978), p. 33.
Auping, Michael. "Judy Pfaff: Turning
Landscape Inside Out." *Arts Magazine*, 57
(September 1982), pp. 74–76.
Saunders, Wade. "Talking Objects:
Interviews with Ten Younger Sculptors."
Art in America, 73 (November 1985),
pp. 130–31.
Schwartz, Ellen. "Artists the Critics Are
Watching." *Art News*, 80 (May 1981),
pp. 79–80.
Smith, Roberta. *Autonomous Objects*
(exhibition catalogue). Charlotte, North
Carolina: Knight Gallery/Spirit Square
Arts Center, 1986.

LARI PITTMAN

Born in Los Angeles, 1952
Studied at the University of California, Los
Angeles (1970–73); California Institute of
the Arts, Valencia (B.F.A., 1974; M.F.A.,
1976)
Lives in Los Angeles

ONE-ARTIST EXHIBITIONS

1982 Los Angeles Contemporary
Exhibitions
1982 Newport Harbor Art Museum,
Newport Beach, California
1983 Rosamund Felsen Gallery,
Los Angeles
1984 Rosamund Felsen Gallery,
Los Angeles
1985 Rosamund Felsen Gallery,
Los Angeles

GROUP EXHIBITIONS

1976 Long Beach City College Art Gallery, California, "Recent Works: Dowell, Pittman, Sherman"
1980 Los Angeles Institute of Contemporary Art, "100 Current Directions in Southern California Art"
1983 Artists Space, New York, "Los Angeles/New York Exchange"
Eaton/Schoen Gallery, San Francisco, "Dealer's Choice: San Francisco/Los Angeles"
Fisher Gallery, University of Southern California, Los Angeles, "Ceci n'est pas le surrealisme, California: Idioms of Surrealism"
Mandeville Art Gallery, University of California, San Diego, "Young American Artists II: Paintings and Painted Wall Reliefs"

BIBLIOGRAPHY

Drohojowska, Hunter. "Lari Pittman." *Art News*, 85 (February 1986), p. 105.
Gardner, Colin. "Lari Pittman." *Flash Art*, 125 (January 1985), pp. 46–47.
Howe, Katherine. "Los Angeles/New York Exchange." *Images & Issues*, 4 (November-December 1983), pp. 56–57.
Larsen, Susan C. "Review." *Artforum*, 21 (May 1983), p. 104.
Mallinson, Constance. "Lari Pittman at Rosamund Felsen." *Art in America*, 73 (February 1985), pp. 144, 147.

RICHARD PRINCE

Born in the Panama Canal Zone, 1949
Lives in New York

ONE-ARTIST EXHIBITIONS

1980 Artists Space, New York
1981 Metro Pictures, New York
Richard Kuhlenschmidt Gallery, Los Angeles
1983 Baskerville + Watson, New York
Institute of Contemporary Arts, London
Le Nouveau Musée, Lyons
1984 Baskerville + Watson, New York
Feature Gallery, Chicago
Riverside Studios, London
1985 International With Monument Gallery, New York
1986 American Fine Arts Company, New York

GROUP EXHIBITIONS

1979 Castelli Graphics, New York, "Pictures: Photographs"
1981 Hayden Gallery, Massachusetts Institute of Technology, Cambridge, "Body Language: Figurative Aspects of Recent Art"
The Kitchen, New York, "Pictures and Promises"
Musée National d'Art Moderne, Centre Georges Pompidou, Paris, "Autoportraits"
1982 Institute of Contemporary Art, University of Pennsylvania, Philadelphia, "Image Scavengers: Photography"
1983 Contemporary Arts Museum, Houston, "The Heroic Figure" (traveled)
1985 The New Museum of Contemporary Art, New York, "The Art of Memory/The Loss of History"
Whitney Museum of American Art, New York, "1985 Biennial Exhibition"
1986 The Biennale of Sydney, Australia
The Queens Museum, Flushing, New York, "The Real Big Picture"

BIBLIOGRAPHY

Crimp, Douglas. "The Photographic Activity of Postmodernism." *October*, 15 (Winter 1980), pp. 91–101.
Grundberg, Andy. "Recycled Images with Eerie Echoes." *The New York Times*, October 21, 1984, p. 16.
Linker, Kate. "On Richard Prince's Photographs." *Arts Magazine*, 57 (November 1982), pp. 120–22.
Robbins, David. "Richard Prince." *Aperture*, 100 (Fall 1985), pp. 6–13.
Smith, Roberta. *Originality, Appropriation, and So Forth* (exhibition catalogue). Sydney, Australia: Art Gallery of New South Wales, 1986.

EDWARD RUSCHA

Born in Omaha, Nebraska, 1937
Studied at Chouinard Art Institute, Los Angeles (1956–60)
Lives in Los Angeles

ONE-ARTIST EXHIBITIONS

1963 Ferus Gallery, Los Angeles
1967 Alexander Iolas Gallery, New York
1968 Irving Blum Gallery, Los Angeles
Galerie Rudolf Zwirner, Cologne
1973 Leo Castelli Gallery, New York
1976 Albright-Knox Art Gallery, Buffalo
Institute of Contemporary Arts, London
1980 Portland Center for the Visual Arts, Oregon
1981 Arco Center for the Visual Arts, Los Angeles
1982 San Francisco Museum of Modern Art (traveled)
1985 Musée Saint Pierre Art Contemporain, Lyons
1986 Westfälischer Kunstverein, Münster, West Germany

GROUP EXHIBITIONS

1962 Pasadena Art Museum, California, "New Paintings of Common Objects"
1963 Los Angeles County Museum of Art, "Six More"
Oakland Art Museum, California, "Pop Art USA"
1967 Whitney Museum of American Art, New York, "1967 Annual Exhibition of Contemporary Painting"
1969 Hayward Gallery, London, "Pop Art"
1970 The Museum of Modern Art, New York, "Information"
1973 Whitney Museum of American Art, New York, "American Drawings 1963–1973"
1978 Albright-Knox Art Gallery, Buffalo, "American Painting of the 1970s" (traveled)
1979 The Art Institute of Chicago, "73rd American Exhibition"
1980 The Museum of Modern Art, New York, "Printed Art: A View of Two Decades"
1981 Los Angeles County Museum of Art, "Art in Los Angeles: Seventeen Artists in the Sixties"
1985 Museum of Art, Fort Lauderdale, "An American Renaissance: Painting and Sculpture Since 1940"

BIBLIOGRAPHY

Alloway, Lawrence. *American Pop Art* (exhibition catalogue). New York: Collier Books in association with the Whitney Museum of American Art, 1974.
Livet, Anne, ed. *The Works of Edward Ruscha* (exhibition catalogue). New York: Hudson Hills Press in association with the San Francisco Museum of Modern Art, 1982. Essays by Dave Hickey and Peter Plagens.
Raspail, Thierry. *Edward Ruscha* (exhibition catalogue). Lyons: Musée Saint Pierre Art Contemporain, 1985. Essays by Peter Schjeldahl and Bernard Brunon.
Stockebrand, Marianne. *4 x 6: Zeichnungen von Edward Ruscha* (exhibition catalogue). Münster, West Germany: Westfälischer Kunstverein, 1986.
Tuchman, Maurice, ed. *Art in Los Angeles: Seventeen Artists in the Sixties* (exhibition catalogue). Los Angeles: Los Angeles County Museum of Art, 1981. Essays by Anne Bartlett Ayres, Susan C. Larsen, Christopher Knight, and Michele D. De Angelus.

ROBERT RYMAN

Born in Nashville, Tennessee, 1930
Studied at Tennessee Polytechnic Institute, Nashville (1948–49); George Peabody College for Teachers, Nashville (1949–50)
Lives in New York

ONE-ARTIST EXHIBITIONS

1969 Fischbach Gallery, New York
1971 Dwan Gallery, New York
1972 John Weber Gallery, New York
The Solomon R. Guggenheim Museum, New York
1974 Stedelijk Museum, Amsterdam

1975 Kunsthalle Basel, Switzerland
1977 Whitechapel Art Gallery, London
1981 Musée National d'Art Moderne,
Centre Georges Pompidou, Paris
1983 Daniel Weinberg Gallery,
Los Angeles
1986 Galerie Maeght Lelong, New York

GROUP EXHIBITIONS

1966 The Solomon R. Guggenheim
Museum, New York, "Systemic Painting"
1969 Kunsthalle Bern, Switzerland, "Live
in Your Head: When Attitude Becomes
Form (Works—Concepts—Processes—
Situations—Information)" (traveled)
Whitney Museum of American Art, New
York, "Anti-Illusion: Procedures/
Materials"
Seattle Art Museum, "557,087" (traveled)
1971 The Solomon R. Guggenheim
Museum, New York, "Sixth Guggenheim
International Exhibition"
1976 Fine Arts Center Gallery, University
of Massachusetts, Amherst, "Three into
Five"
1978 Albright-Knox Art Gallery, Buffalo,
"American Painting of the 1970s"
(traveled)
1981 Royal Academy of Arts, London,
"A New Spirit in Painting"
1984 Stedelijk Museum, Amsterdam,
"La Grande Parade"
Whitney Museum of American Art, New
York, "American Art Since 1970:
Painting, Sculpture, and Drawings from
the Collection of the Whitney Museum
of American Art" (traveled)
1985 Museum of Art, Carnegie Institute,
Pittsburgh, "1985 Carnegie
International"
The Museum of Modern Art, New York,
"New Works on Paper 3"

BIBLIOGRAPHY

Davies, Hugh M., ed. *Critical Perspectives in
American Art* (exhibition catalogue).
Amherst, Massachusetts: Fine Arts
Center Gallery, University of
Massachusetts, 1976. Essays by Sam
Hunter, Rosalind Krauss, and Marcia
Tucker.
Perrone, Jeff. "Robert Ryman." *Artforum*, 17
(March 1979), pp. 61–62.
Sauer, Christel. *Robert Ryman Paintings
1958–80* (exhibition catalogue). Zurich:
Halle für Internationale Neue Kunst,
1980.
Tuchman, Phyllis. "An Interview with
Robert Ryman." *Artforum*, 9 (May 1971),
pp. 70–73.
Waldman, Diane. *Robert Ryman* (exhibition
catalogue). New York: The Solomon R.
Guggenheim Museum, 1972.

ALAN SARET

Born in New York, 1944
Studied at Cornell University, Ithaca,
New York (B.A., 1966)
Lives in New York

ONE-ARTIST EXHIBITIONS

1968 Bykert Gallery, New York
1974 The Clocktower, Institute for Art and
Urban Resources, New York
1979 University Art Museum, University
of California, Berkeley
1980 Charles Cowles Gallery, New York
1981 Galerie Rudolf Zwirner, Cologne
1982 Nigel Greenwood Gallery, London
Newport Harbor Art Museum, Newport
Beach, California
1983 Daniel Weinberg Gallery,
Los Angeles
Albright-Knox Art Gallery, Buffalo
1986 Margo Leavin Gallery, Los Angeles

GROUP EXHIBITIONS

1969 Leo Castelli Gallery, New York,
"Nine in a Warehouse"
1975 Art Park, Lewiston, New York,
"The Ghosthouse"
1977 Museum of Contemporary Art,
Chicago, "View of a Decade"
1979 The Museum of Modern Art, New
York, "Contemporary Sculpture:
Selections from the Collection of the
Museum of Modern Art"
1981 Whitney Museum of American Art,
New York, "Developments in Recent
Sculpture"
1986 Hayden Gallery, Massachusetts
Institute of Technology, Cambridge,
"Natural Forms and Forces"
Palacio Velázquez, Madrid, "Between
Geometry and Gesture: American
Sculpture 1965–1975"

BIBLIOGRAPHY

Armstrong, Richard. "Alan Saret, Daniel
Weinberg Gallery." *Artforum*, 18
(February 1980), pp. 106–07.
Baker, Kenneth. "Alan Saret at the
Albright-Knox and Hallwalls." *Art in
America*, 71 (May 1983), p. 177.
Crary, Jonathan. "Alan Saret." *Arts
Magazine*, 52 (September 1977), p. 4.
Kertess, Klaus. *Matter into Aether* (exhibition
catalogue). Newport Beach, California:
Newport Harbor Art Museum, 1982.
Marshall, Richard. *Developments in Recent
Sculpture* (exhibition catalogue). New
York: Whitney Museum of American
Art, 1981.
Wasserman, Emily. "Alan Saret, Bykert
Gallery." *Artforum*, 6 (January 1969),
p. 59.

JULIAN SCHNABEL

Born in New York, 1951
Studied at the University of Houston
(B.F.A., 1972); Independent Study
Program, Whitney Museum of American
Art, New York (1973–74)
Lives in New York

ONE-ARTIST EXHIBITIONS

1976 Contemporary Arts Museum,
Houston
1979 Mary Boone Gallery, New York
Daniel Weinberg Gallery, San Francisco
1981 Mary Boone Gallery, New York
Leo Castelli Gallery, New York
1982 Stedlijk Museum, Amsterdam
The Tate Gallery, London
1983 Leo Castelli Gallery, New York
1984 The Pace Gallery, New York
1986 The Pace Gallery, New York
Whitechapel Art Gallery, London
(traveled)

GROUP EXHIBITIONS

1977 Renaissance Society at the University
of Chicago, "Visionary Images"
1980 Venice, Italy, "XXXIX Biennale di
Venezia"
1981 Hayden Gallery, Massachusetts
Institute of Technology, Cambridge,
"Body Language: Figurative Aspects of
Recent Art"
Museen der Stadt Köln, Cologne,
"Westkunst"
The Royal Academy, London, "A New
Spirit in Painting"
Whitney Museum of American Art, New
York, "1981 Biennial Exhibition"
1982 Martin Gropius-Bau, West Berlin,
"Zeitgeist"
1983 The Museum of Contemporary Art,
Los Angeles, "The First Show"
Whitney Museum of American Art, New
York, "1983 Biennial Exhibition"
1986 The Art Institute of Chicago, "The
Seventy-fifth American Exhibition"

BIBLIOGRAPHY

Bleckner, Ross. "Transcendent Anti-
Fetishism." *Artforum*, 7 (March 1979),
pp. 50–55.
Kuspit, Donald. "The Rhetoric of Rawness:
Its Effects on Meaning in Julian
Schnabel's Paintings." *Arts Magazine*, 59
(March 1985), pp. 126–30.
McEvilley, Thomas. *Julian Schnabel: Paintings
1975–1986* (exhibition catalogue).
London: Whitechapel Art Gallery, 1986.
McGuigan, Cathleen. "Julian Schnabel: 'I
Always Knew It Would Be Like This.'"
Art News, 81 (Summer 1982), pp. 88–94.
Ricard, René. "Not About Julian Schnabel."
Artforum, 19 (Summer 1981), pp. 74–80.

THE STARN TWINS
DOUGLAS STARN
MICHAEL STARN

Born in Northfield, New Jersey, 1961
Studied at the School of the Museum of
Fine Arts, Boston (B.F.A., 1985)
Live in Boston

TWO-ARTIST EXHIBITIONS

1985 Stux Gallery, Boston
1986 Institute of Contemporary Art,
Boston
Stux Gallery, New York

GROUP EXHIBITIONS

1985 Carpenter Center for the Visual Arts,
Harvard University, Cambridge,
Massachusetts, "New Work from
New York"
Institute of Contemporary Art, Boston,
"Boston Now: Photography"
Museum of Fine Arts, Boston, "Museum
School Travelling Scholars"
1986 Massimo Audiello Gallery, New York,
"Group Exhibition"
Faneuil Hall, Boston, "Salute to Boston
Artists"
Rose Art Museum, Brandeis University,
Waltham, Massachusetts, "The Joseph
Mascheck Collection of Contemporary
Art"

BIBLIOGRAPHY

Frick, Thomas. "The Starn Twins at Stux."
Art in America, 73 (November 1985),
p. 168.
Indiana, Gary. "Imitation of Life." The
Village Voice, April 29, 1986, pp. 87–88.
Koslow, Francine A. "Doubling
Photograph: The Starn Twins." Print
Collector's Newsletter, 17 (November-
December 1986), pp. 163–66.
Mascheck, Joseph. "Of One Mind: Photos
by the Starn Twins of Boston." Arts
Magazine, 60 (March 1986), pp. 69–71.

DONALD SULTAN

Born in Asheville, North Carolina, 1951
Studied at the University of North
Carolina, Chapel Hill (B.F.A., 1973);
School of the Art Institute of Chicago
(M.F.A., 1975)
Lives in New York

ONE-ARTIST EXHIBITIONS

1976 N.A.M.E. Gallery, Chicago
1977 Artists Space, New York
1979 Willard Gallery, New York
1981 Daniel Weinberg Gallery,
San Francisco
1982 Blum Helman Gallery, New York
1983 Akira Ikeda Gallery, Tokyo
1984 Blum Helman Gallery, New York

1985 Gian Enzo Sperone, Rome
1986 Blum Helman Gallery, New York
Museum of Contemporary Art, Chicago
(traveled)

GROUP EXHIBITIONS

1978 The New Museum of Contemporary
Art, New York, "Doubletake"
1979 Whitney Museum of American Art,
New York, "1979 Biennial Exhibition"
Renaissance Society at the University of
Chicago, "Visionary Images"
1981 Contemporary Arts Museum,
Houston, "The Americans: The
Landscape"
1982 Indianapolis Museum of Art,
"Paintings and Sculpture Today: 1982"
1983 The Museum of Modern Art, New
York, "Prints from Blocks: Gauguin
to Now"
1984 The Museum of Modern Art, New
York, "An International Survey of Recent
Painting and Sculpture"
Artists Space, New York, "A Decade of
New Art"
1985 Aspen Art Museum, Colorado,
"American Paintings 1975–1985:
Selections from the Collection of Aron
and Phyllis Katz"
1986 The Brooklyn Museum, New York,
"Monumental Drawings: Works by
Twenty-two Contemporary Americans"

BIBLIOGRAPHY

Levin, Kim. "Donald Sultan and Lois
Lane." Flash Art, 101 (January-February
1981), pp. 49–50.
Russell, John. "Donald Sultan." The New
York Times, April 30, 1982, p. C24.
Tucker, Marcia. Four Artists: Drawings
(exhibition catalogue). New York: The
New Museum of Contemporary Art,
1977.
Zimmer, William. "Artbreakers: Donald
Sultan." Soho Weekly News, September 17,
1980.

PHILIP TAAFFE

Born in Elizabeth, New Jersey, 1955
Studied at the Cooper Union, New York
(B.F.A., 1977)
Lives in New York

ONE-ARTIST EXHIBITIONS

1982 Roger Litz Gallery, New York
1984 Galerie Ascan Crone, Hamburg
Pat Hearn Gallery, New York
1986 Pat Hearn Gallery, New York
Galerie Ascan Crone, Hamburg
Galerie Paul Maenz, Cologne

GROUP EXHIBITIONS

1983 Studio Sandro Chia, New York,
"Turn It Over"

1984 Cable Gallery, New York, "Sex"
Massimo Audiello Gallery, New York,
"The Chi-Chi Show"
Wolff Gallery, New York, "Post Style"
Wacoal Art Center, Tokyo, "Vernacular
Abstraction"
1985 Charlottenborg Exhibition Hall,
Copenhagen, "A Brave New World: A
New Generation"
1986 John Good Gallery, New York,
"Recent Abstract Painting"
Centre National d'Art Contemporain,
Nice, France, "Tableau Abstraits"
Tony Shafrazi Gallery, New York, "What
It Is"
Fundació Caixa de Pensiones, Barcelona,
"L'Art i el Seu Doble. Panorama de l'Art
a Nova York"

BIBLIOGRAPHY

Cameron, Dan. "The Other Philip Taaffe."
Arts Magazine, 60 (October 1985),
pp. 18–20.
Cortez, Diego. Philip Taaffe (exhibition
catalogue). Hamburg: Galerie Ascan
Crone, 1986.
Kohn, Michael. "Philip Taaffe." Flash Art,
no. 124 (October-November 1985),
pp. 72–73.
Smith, Roberta. "Art and Its Double." The
Village Voice, November 7, 1984, p. 45.
————. Vernacular Abstraction (exhibition
catalogue). Tokyo: Wacoal Art Center,
1985.
Solomon, Thomas. A Brave New World: A
New Generation (exhibition catalogue).
Copenhagen: Charlottenborg Exhibition
Hall, 1985.

RICHARD TUTTLE

Born in Rahway, New Jersey, 1941
Studied at Trinity College, Hartford,
Connecticut (B.A., 1963)
Lives in New York

ONE-ARTIST EXHIBITIONS

1965 Betty Parsons Gallery, New York
1968 Betty Parsons Gallery, New York
1969 Nicholas Wilder Gallery, Los Angeles
1972 The Museum of Modern Art,
New York
1974 Nigel Greenwood Gallery, London
1975 Whitney Museum of American Art,
New York (traveled)
1978 Young Hoffman Gallery, Chicago
1979 Stedelijk Museum, Amsterdam
1983 Blum Helman Gallery, New York
1984 Daniel Weinberg Gallery,
Los Angeles
1985 Städtisches Museum Abteiberg
Mönchengladbach, West Germany
Institute of Contemporary Arts, London

GROUP EXHIBITIONS

1969 Kunsthalle Bern, Switzerland, "Live in Your Head: When Attitudes Become Form (Works—Concepts—Processes—Situations—Information)" (traveled)
Whitney Museum of American Art, New York, "Anti-Illusion: Procedures/Materials"
1974 The Art Museum, Princeton University, Princeton, New Jersey, "Line as Language: Six Artists Draw"
1975 The Baltimore Museum of Art, "14 Artists"
1977 Museum of Contemporary Art, Chicago, "A View of a Decade"
1980 Hayward Gallery, London, "Pier & Ocean: Construction in the Art of the Seventies" (traveled)
1982 Blum Helman Gallery, New York, "Ryman/Tuttle/Twombly: New Work"
1985 Whitney Museum of American Art, New York, "Drawing Acquisitions: 1981–1985"

BIBLIOGRAPHY

Cooke, Lynne. "Richard Tuttle at Victoria Miro." *Artscribe International*, 58 (June-July 1986), p. 73.
Graevenitz, Gerhard von. *Pier & Ocean: Construction in the Art of the Seventies* (exhibition catalogue). London: Hayward Gallery, 1980.
Krauss, Rosalind. *Line as Language: Six Artists Draw* (exhibition catalogue). Princeton, New Jersey: The Art Museum, Princeton University, 1974.
Larsen, Susan C. "Richard Tuttle, Daniel Weinberg Gallery." *Artforum*, 24 (December 1985), pp. 93–94.
Pincus-Witten, Robert. "The Art of Richard Tuttle." *Artforum*, 8 (February 1970), pp. 62–67.
Tucker, Marcia. *Richard Tuttle* (exhibition catalogue). New York: Whitney Museum of American Art, 1975.
Tuttle, Richard. *Richard Tuttle: Paris* (exhibition catalogue). Calais, France: Musée de Calais, 1982.

BRUCE WEBER

Born in Greensburg, Pennsylvania, 1946
Studied at Denison University, Granville, Ohio (1965–67); New York University (1967–68); The New School, New York (1970)
Lives in New York

ONE-ARTIST EXHIBITIONS

1974 Razor Gallery, New York
1984 Robert Miller Gallery, New York
Olympus Centre, London
Galerie Texbraun, Paris
1986 Fraenkel Gallery, San Francisco
Kunsthalle Basel, Switzerland
Robert Miller Gallery, New York
Fay Gold Gallery, Atlanta

GROUP EXHIBITIONS

1982 The Grey Art Gallery and Study Center, New York University, "Faces Photographed"
Staley Wise Gallery, New York, "Men in Fashion"
1985 Museum für Kunst und Kulturgeschichte der Stadt Dortmund, West Germany, "Das Aktfoto"
Victoria and Albert Museum, London, "Shots of Style"

BIBLIOGRAPHY

Ammann, Jean-Christophe. *Bruce Weber* (exhibition catalogue). Basel, Switzerland: Kunsthalle Basel, 1986.
Bailey, David. *Shots of Style* (exhibition catalogue). London: Victoria and Albert Museum, 1985.
Cheim, John E., ed. *Bruce Weber*. Pasadena, California: Twelvetrees Press, 1983.
Ellenzweig, Allen. "Bruce Weber at Robert Miller." *Art in America*, 72 (November 1984), pp. 163–64.
Smith, Paul. "Bruce Weber's Athletic Fashion." *Arts Magazine*, 58 (Summer 1984), pp. 126–27.
Weber, Bruce. *O Rio de Janeiro*. New York: Alfred A. Knopf, 1986.

GRAHAME WEINBREN AND ROBERTA FRIEDMAN

GRAHAME WEINBREN

Born in Johannesburg, South Africa, 1947
Lives in New York

ROBERTA FRIEDMAN

Born in New York, 1948
Studied at the State University of New York, College at Buffalo (B.A., 1971); California Institute of the Arts, Valencia (M.F.A., 1973)
Lives in New York

TWO-ARTIST EXHIBITIONS

1979 Newport Harbor Art Museum, Newport Beach, California
1980 Edinburgh International Film Festival
Institute of Contemporary Arts, London
The Kitchen, New York
Stedelijk Museum, Amsterdam
1981 Millennium, New York
1983 Museum of Art, Carnegie Institute, Pittsburgh
Collective for Living Cinema, New York
1986 The Museum of Contemporary Art, Los Angeles
Walker Art Center, Minneapolis

GROUP EXHIBITIONS

1974 Los Angeles Film Exposition
1975 Long Beach Museum of Art, California, "Southland Video Anthology"
1976 Wellington Film Festival, New Zealand
1979 Film London
Sinking Creek Film Celebration, Tennessee
1980 The Kitchen, "Filmworks"
San Francisco Art Institute Film Festival
1981 Teatro del Falcone, Genoa, Italy, "Il Gergo Inquieto"
1983 American Film Institute, Washington, D.C. and Los Angeles, "National Video Festival"
The Kitchen, New York, "Filmworks"

BIBLIOGRAPHY

Stern, Leslie. "Point of View: The Blind Spot." *Film Reader*, no. 4 (1979), pp. 214–36.
Weinbren, Grahame. "Film Space: An Outline Study." *Millennium Film Journal*, no. 16/17/18 (Winter 1986–87), pp. 328–35.
————. "Selective Transparencies: Pat O'Neill's Recent Films." *Millennium Film Journal*, no. 6 (Spring 1980), pp. 50–72.
————. "Taking Up Space: Brakhage, Snow, and David Wilson." *Los Angeles Institute of Contemporary Art Journal*, no. 29 (Summer 1981), pp. 48–54.
————, and C. Noll Brinckmann. "Mutations of Film Narrative." *Idiolects*, no. 12 (Fall 1982), pp. 22–36.

TERRY WINTERS

Born in New York, 1949
Studied at Pratt Institute, Brooklyn, New York (B.F.A., 1971)
Lives in New York

ONE-ARTIST EXHIBITIONS

1982 Sonnabend Gallery, New York
1983 Karen and Jean Bernier Gallery, Athens
Reed College, Portland
1984 Sonnabend Gallery, New York
Daniel Weinberg Gallery, Los Angeles
1985 Kunstmuseum Luzern, Switzerland
1986 Castelli Graphics, New York
Barbara Krakow Gallery, Boston
Sonnabend Gallery, New York
The Tate Gallery, London

GROUP EXHIBITIONS

1977 The Drawing Center, New York, "Summer/77"
P.S. 1, Institute for Art and Urban Resources, Long Island City, New York, "A Painting Show"
1981 Delahunty Gallery, Dallas, "Committed to Paint"
1983 Hayden Gallery, Massachusetts Institute of Technology, Cambridge, "Affinities"
The Tate Gallery, London, "New Art"

1984 The Museum of Modern Art, New York, "An International Survey of Recent Painting and Sculpture"
Renaissance Society at the University of Chicago, "The Meditative Surface"
1985 Whitney Museum of American Art, New York, "1985 Biennial Exhibition"
1986 Museum of Art, Fort Lauderdale, "An American Renaissance: Painting and Sculpture Since 1940"
The Brooklyn Museum, New York, "Monumental Drawings: Works by Twenty-two Contemporary Americans"

BIBLIOGRAPHY

Carlson, Prudence. "Terry Winters' Earthly Anecdotes." *Artforum*, 23 (November 1984), pp. 65–68.
Hughes, Robert. "Art: Obliquely Addressing Nature." *Time*, February 24, 1986, p. 83.
Kertess, Klaus, and Martin Kunz. *Terry Winters* (exhibition catalogue). Lucerne, Switzerland: Kunstmuseum Luzern, 1985.
Lewison, Jeremy. *Terry Winters' Eight Paintings* (exhibition catalogue). London: The Tate Gallery, 1986.
Liebmann, Lisa. "Terry Winters, Sonnabend Gallery." *Artforum*, 21 (February 1983), p. 72.

FILM AND VIDEO

ERICKA BECKMAN

Born in Hempstead, New York, 1951
Studied at Washington University, St. Louis (B.F.A., 1974); Independent Study Program, Whitney Museum of American Art, New York (1975); California Institute of the Arts, Valencia (M.F.A., 1976)
Lives in New York

ONE-ARTIST EXHIBITIONS

1982 Boston Film/Video Foundation
Media Study, Buffalo
1983 The Kitchen, New York
Millennium, New York
1984 Institute of Contemporary Arts, London
Los Angeles Contemporary Exhibitions
Pacific Film Archive, University Art Museum, University of California, Berkeley
1985 The New Museum of Contemporary Art, New York
1986 Hallwalls, Buffalo
Walker Art Center, Minneapolis

GROUP EXHIBITIONS

1981 Anthology Film Archives, New York, "Super-8 Survey"
Bleecker Street Cinema, New York, "Super-8 Series"
1983 Lincoln Center for the Performing Arts, New York, "The Twenty-first New York Film Festival"
Whitney Museum of American Art, New York, "1983 Biennial Exhibition" (traveled)
1984 International With Monument Gallery, New York, "Still Life with Transaction"
Wadsworth Atheneum, Hartford, Connecticut, "Women as Directors" (traveled)
1985 Musée National d'Art Moderne, Centre Georges Pompidou, Paris, "Alibi"
Kunstmuseum Bern, Switzerland, "Das Poetisch ABC"
1986 The Kitchen, New York, "Bette Gordon and Ericka Beckman"
Palais des Beaux-Arts, Brussels, "Au Coeur du Maelstrom"

BIBLIOGRAPHY

Banes, Sally. "Imagination and Play: The Films of Ericka Beckman." *Millennium Film Journal*, no. 13 (Fall-Winter 1983–84), pp. 98–112.
Beckman, Ericka. "Drawings for *You the Better*." In *Cave Canem*, edited by John Miller. New York: Cave Canem Books, 1983.
Hoberman, J. "A Kind of Close Encounter." *The Village Voice*, December 13, 1983, p. 76.
Rickey, Carrie. "Popcorn and Canvas." *Artforum*, 22 (December 1983), pp. 64–69.
Sitney, P. Adams. "Point of View: Rear-Garde." *American Film*, 10 (July-August 1985), pp. 13, 61.

JAMES BENNING

Born in Milwaukee, 1942
Studied at the University of Wisconsin, Milwaukee (B.S., 1966; M.F.A., 1975)
Lives in New York

ONE-ARTIST EXHIBITIONS

1973 Film Forum, New York
1975 Museum of Contemporary Art, Chicago
1978 Albright-Knox Art Gallery, Buffalo
San Francisco Museum of Modern Art
1980 The Museum of Modern Art, New York
1984 The Museum of Fine Arts, Houston
1985 The Kitchen, New York
1986 Millennium, New York
Walker Art Center, Minneapolis
Whitney Museum of American Art, New York

GROUP EXHIBITIONS

1974 Cannes Film Festival
1975 The Museum of Modern Art, New York, "New Directors/New Films"
1977 Kassel, West Germany, "Documenta 6"
West Berlin, "Internationales Forum des Jungen Films"
1978 Art Park, Lewiston, New York
Edinburgh International Film Festival
1979 Whitney Museum of American Art, New York, "1979 Biennial Exhibition" (traveled)
1981 Whitney Museum of American Art, New York, "1981 Biennial Exhibition" (traveled)
1983 Whitney Museum of American Art, New York, "1983 Biennial Exhibition" (traveled)

BIBLIOGRAPHY

Benning, James. "Sound and Stills from *Grand Opera*." *October*, 12 (Spring 1980), pp. 22–45.
Dieckmann, Katherine. "Disturbances in the Field." *The Village Voice*, November 4, 1986, p. 72.
Hanhardt, John G. "James Benning" (program notes). *The New American Filmmakers Series* 31. New York: Whitney Museum of American Art, 1986.
MacDonald, Scott. "An Interview with James Benning." *Afterimage*, 9 (December 1981), pp. 12–19.
Taubin, Amy. "Eleven by Fourteen." *Soho Weekly News*, April 28, 1977, p. 72.

ALAN BERLINER

Born in New York, 1956
Studied at the State University of New York at Binghamton (B.A., 1977); University of Oklahoma, Norman (M.F.A., 1979)
Lives in New York

ONE-ARTIST EXHIBITIONS

1977 Collective for Living Cinema, New York
1982 Colgate University, Hamilton, New York
Collective for Living Cinema, New York
1984 Hunter College, New York
1986 Berks Filmmakers, Reading, Pennsylvania
California Institute of the Arts, Valencia
Millennium, New York
Pacific Film Archive, University Art Museum, University of California, Berkeley
San Francisco Cinémathèque

GROUP EXHIBITIONS

1980 Hunter College, New York, "Frames: Two-Dimensional Work by Film Artists"

1982 Bleecker Street Cinema, New York, "Film Pulse"
Collective for Living Cinema, New York "Ten Years of Living Cinema"
The Queens Museum, Flushing, New York, "Cinéma Trouve"
1984 A.I.R. Gallery, New York, "Artist as Filmmaker"
WNYC-TV, New York, "Garden of Eden"
1986 Munson-Williams-Proctor Institute, Utica, New York, "Frames of Mind"

BIBLIOGRAPHY

Beroes, Stephanie. "Interviews/New York." *Cinematograph*, 2 (November 1986), pp. 57–59.
Johnson, William. "The Liberation of Echo: A New Hearing for Film Sound." *Film Quarterly*, 38 (Summer 1985), p. 11.
Rice, Shelley. "Reviews: 'Frames.'" *Artforum*, 18 (Summer 1980), pp. 88–89.

STEPHANIE BEROES

Born in Pittsburgh, 1954
Studied at the University of Pittsburgh (B.A., 1975); San Francisco Art Institute (M.F.A., 1978)
Lives in New York

ONE-ARTIST EXHIBITIONS

1979 Pittsburgh Filmmakers
1980 Chicago Filmmakers
Kommunales Kino, Frankfurt
Millennium, New York
San Francisco Cinémathèque
1981 Berks Filmmakers, Reading, Pennsylvania
1984 Perihelion Gallery, Milwaukee
1986 Collective for Living Cinema, New York
Filmforum, Los Angeles
San Francisco Cinémathèque

GROUP EXHIBITIONS

1975 School of the Art Institute of Chicago, "Best Films from Experimental 5, Knokke Le Zeist" (traveled)
1976 San Francisco Cinémathèque, "New Filmmakers"
1977 Pacific Film Archive, University Art Museum, University of California, Berkeley, "Best Films from Intercat Film Festival" (traveled)
1979 British Film Institute, London, "Third International Avant-Garde Festival"
1980 Hirshhorn Museum and Sculpture Garden, Smithsonian Institution, Washington, D.C., "New Films Showcase"
Institute of Contemporary Arts, London, "Women's Only Festival"
The Neighborhood Film Project, Philadelphia, "New Films"
1981 Spiele, West Berlin, "31st International Film Festival"

1983 Milwaukee Filmmakers Festival
1986 Minneapolis College of Art and Design, "Films by Women"

BIBLIOGRAPHY

Fischer, Lucy. "Visiting Filmmaker Stephanie Beroes Presents Her Films *Valley Fever, Recital,* and *Debt Begins At 20*" (program notes). Pittsburgh: Museum of Art, Carnegie Institute, 1980.
Locke, Stephen. "Aufregende Konzeption." *TIP,* 12 (June 20, 1980), p. 46.
Marchetti, Gina. "Documenting Punk: A Subcultural Investigation." *Film Reader Journal,* 4 (Spring 1982), pp. 269–80.
Rosenbaum, Jonathan. "Barcelona Boogie and Pittsburgh Punk." *Soho Weekly News,* June 4, 1980, p. 36.
Sterritt, David. "The Dream Screen: On Being Female in the 20th Century." *The Christian Science Monitor,* November 5, 1983, p. 23.

PEER BODE

Born in Rosenheim, West Germany, 1952
Studied at the State University of New York at Binghamton (B.A., 1974); State University of New York, College at Buffalo (M.A., 1978)
Lives in Owego, New York

ONE-ARTIST EXHIBITIONS

1976 Everson Museum of Art of Syracuse and Onondaga County, Syracuse, New York
Herbert F. Johnson Museum of Art, Ithaca, New York
1977 Arnolfini Arts Center, Rhinebeck, New York
1979 The Museum of Modern Art, New York
School of Visual Arts, New York
1980 Experimental Television Center, Owego, New York
1982 School of the Art Institute of Chicago
1984 Media Study, Buffalo
1985 Carnegie Cultural Center, North Tonawanda, New York
1986 State University of New York at Binghamton

GROUP EXHIBITIONS

1980 15th Annual Avant-Garde Festival, New York
1982 State University of New York at Binghamton, "Festival of Contemporary Art"
1984 Hallwalls, Buffalo, "Signals as Instruments"
West Coast University, Los Angeles, "Computer and Art Education and Research"
1985 The Bronx Museum of the Arts, New York, "Emerging Expression: The Artist and Computer"
Limbo Lounge, New York, "Techno-Bop"

1986 American Film Institute, Washington, D.C. and Los Angeles, "National Video Festival"
Arnot Art Museum, Elmira, New York, "Generic Real-Time Interactive Digital"
The Katonah Gallery, Katonah, New York, "A Video Primer: Electronic Art from the Eighties"

BIBLIOGRAPHY

Chamberlain, Peter, ed. *Generic Real-Time Interactive Digital* (exhibition catalogue). Elmira, New York: Arnot Art Museum, 1986. Essays by Peer Bode, John Driscoll, Phillip Edelstein, Ralph Hocking, and Curt Dunnam.
Gever, Martha. "Traveling Light: CAPS Video Goes National." *Afterimage,* 9 (April 1982), pp. 8–9.
Sundell, Nina. *CAPS/ICI 1981 Traveling Video Festival* (exhibition catalogue). New York: Independent Curators Incorporated, 1981.

JOAN BRADERMAN

Born in Washington, D.C., 1948
Studied at Harvard University, Cambridge, Massachusetts (B.A., 1970); New York University (M.A., 1973; M. Phil., 1976)
Lives in Northampton, Massachusetts, and New York

ONE-ARTIST EXHIBITIONS

1983 Feminist Art Institute, New York
1984 The Kitchen, New York
Vandam Theater, New York
1985 Brown University, Providence, Rhode Island
California Institute of the Arts, Valencia
1986 University of Massachusetts, Amherst

GROUP EXHIBITIONS

1984 American Film Institute, National Video Festival Olympic Screenings, Los Angeles and Washington, D.C., "Thinking Television: Low-Tech Representations"
A.I.R. Gallery, New York, "Current Issues in Video"
Walker Art Center, Minneapolis, "Paper Tiger Television"
Washington Project for the Arts Gallery, Washington, D.C., "The Magazine Stand: Photography, Design, Paintings and Installations on the Subject of Mass Media"
1985 Whitney Museum of American Art, New York, "Paper Tiger Television"
Women in Film and Video, Boston, "Made for TV" (conference)
1986 American Film Institute, Washington D.C. and Los Angeles, "National Video Festival"
Boston Film/Video Foundation, "Joan Braderman and Manuel De Landa"

Institute of Contemporary Art, Boston, "Mediated Narrative"
Cinemama, Montreal, "Love and Language"

BIBLIOGRAPHY

Braderman, Joan. "Joan Does Dynasty: A Neopagan, Postsituationist, Social/Anarcho/Feminist Expose" (script). *The Independent*, 9 (August-September 1986), pp. 14–19.
———. "Juggling Contradiction: Feminism, The Individual and What's Left." *Heresies: A Feminist Publication on Art and Politics*, 1 (January 1977), pp. 88–93.
———. "Report: The First Festival of Women's Films." *Artforum*, 11 (September 1972), pp. 86–92.
Gever, Martha. "Meet the Press: On Paper Tiger Television." *Afterimage*, 11 (November 1983), pp. 7–11.
Lord, Catherine. "Thinking Television: Low-Tech Representations." In *National Video Festival Olympic Screenings* (exhibition catalogue). Los Angeles and Washington, D.C.: American Film Institute, 1984.

HANS BREDER

Born in Herford, Germany, 1935
Studied with Woldemar Winkler, Gütersloh, West Germany (1953–55); Hochschule für Bildende Künste, Hamburg (1961–64)
Lives in Iowa City

ONE-ARTIST EXHIBITIONS

1967 Richard L. Feigen & Co., New York
1969 Richard L. Feigen & Co., New York
1972 Richard L. Feigen, Chicago
Galerie Marcel Liatowitsch, Basel, Switzerland
1975 The Kitchen, New York
1976 Internationaal Cultureel Centrum, Antwerp
Studentski Kulturni Center, Beograd, Yugoslavia
1979 Galerie Wolfgang Förster, Münster, West Germany
1982 Galerie Hachmeister and Schnake, Münster, West Germany
1983 P.S. 1, Institute for Art and Urban Resources, Long Island City, New York

GROUP EXHIBITIONS

1967 Whitney Museum of American Art, New York, "Recent Acquisitions"
1969 La Jolla Museum of Contemporary Art, California, "Affect/Effect"
1972 Max Hutchinson Gallery, New York, "Hybrids"
1982 Interactive Satellite Teleconference, Iowa City—New York—Los Angeles, "The Artist and Television."
1984 The Museum of Modern Art, New York, "Recent Acquisitions"

1985 Time-Based Arts, Amsterdam, "Talking Back to the Media"
1986 Los Angeles Contemporary Exhibitions, "Video and Language :: Video as Language"
Galerie Remberti, Bremen, West Germany, "Konstruktiv"
2nd Videonale, Bonn

BIBLIOGRAPHY

Breder, Hans. *Portrait of Rosa*. New York: Chicago Books, 1983.
———, and Stephen Foster. *Intermedia*. Iowa City: The University of Iowa Press, 1979.
Foster, Stephen, and Estera Milman. "The Media as Medium: Hans Breder's Berlin Work." *Kansas Quarterly*, 17, no. 3 (1985), pp. 17–24.
Herzogenrath, Wulf. *Video Kunst in Deutschland 1963–1982*. Stuttgart: Verlag Gerd Hatje, 1982.
Wooster, Ann-Sargent. "Manhattan Short Cuts: Hans Breder/Portrait of Rosa." *Afterimage*, 10 (January 1983), pp. 16–17.

JUAN DOWNEY

Born in Santiago, Chile, 1940
Studied at the Catholic University of Chile, Santiago (B. Arch., 1964) Atelier 17, Paris (1963–65); Pratt Institute, Brooklyn, New York (1967–69)
Lives in New York

ONE-ARTIST EXHIBITIONS

1968 Judson Church Gallery, New York
1970 Howard Wise Gallery, New York
1974 The Kitchen, New York
1975 Anthology Film Archives, New York
1976 Long Beach Museum of Art, California
1977 Everson Museum of Art of Syracuse and Onondaga County, Syracuse, New York
1978 Whitney Museum of American Art, New York
1983 P.S. 1, Institute for Art and Urban Resources, Long Island City, New York
1984 Galeria Plastica 3, Santiago, Chile
San Francisco Museum of Modern Art

GROUP EXHIBITIONS

1968 The Brooklyn Museum, New York, "Some More Beginnings"
1974 John F. Kennedy Center for the Performing Arts, Washington, D.C., "Art Now '74"
Kölnischer Kunstverein, Cologne, "Projekt '74"
1977 Kassel, West Germany, "Documenta 6"
1980 Venice, Italy, "XXXIX Biennale di Venezia" (traveled)
1983 Whitney Museum of American Art, New York, "1983 Biennial Exhibition" (traveled)

1984 The Museum of Modern Art, New York, "A Survey: Artist's TV Lab, WNET/Thirteen"
1985 American Film Institute, Washington, D.C. and Los Angeles, "National Video Festival"
Whitney Museum of American Art, New York, "1985 Biennial Exhibition" (traveled)

BIBLIOGRAPHY

Ballerini, Julia. "Review of Exhibitions: Juan Downey at Schlesinger-Boisanté." *Art in America*, 70 (November 1982), pp. 123–24.
Boyle, Deirdre. "Juan Downey's Recent Videotapes." *Afterimage*, 6 (Summer 1978), pp. 10–11.
Downey, Juan. "Travelogues of Video Trans Americas." In *Video Art: An Anthology*, edited by Ira Schneider and Beryl Korot. New York: Harcourt, Brace, Jovanovich, 1976, pp. 38–39.
Ffrench-Frazier, Nina. "Juan Downey: Chilean Ulysses." *Artweek*, March 13, 1976, p. 13.
Wooster, Ann-Sargent. "Juan Downey's Looking Glass." *Afterimage*, 10 (Summer 1982), pp. 24–27.

STEVE FAGIN

Born in Chicago, 1946
Studied at Northwestern University, Evanston, Illinois (M.A., 1973)
Lives in Richmond, California

ONE-ARTIST EXHIBITIONS

1985 Anthology Film Archives, New York
School of the Art Institute of Chicago
Yale University, New Haven
1986 Brown University, Providence, Rhode Island
Film in the Cities, St. Paul, Minnesota
The Kitchen, New York
The Museum of Modern Art, New York
San Francisco Cinémathèque
Video Free America, San Francisco

GROUP EXHIBITIONS

1984 The Kitchen, New York, "Video Viewing Room"
1985 Co-lab, San Francisco, "Video Refusées"
The Hague, The Netherlands, "World-Wide Video Festival"
The Museum of Modern Art, New York, "West Coast Video"
Rotterdam Film Festival
1986 American Film Institute, Washington, D.C. and Los Angeles, "National Video Festival"

BIBLIOGRAPHY

Kamphuizen, Henny. "Virtual Play: The Double Direct Monkey Wrench in Black's Machinery." *Videoline*, no. 1 (September 1986), pp. 19–23.

Kruger, Barbara. "Reviews. Steve Fagin: 'Virtual Play,' The Kitchen." *Artforum*, 23 (March 1985), pp. 98–99.

Magiera, Mark. "Virtual Play Plays Seriously." *Mindport*, 1 (Fall 1985), pp. 4–5.

Morse, Margaret. "Waking and Shaking." *Afterimage*, 13 (November 1985), pp. 15–17.

ERNIE GEHR

Born in Wisconsin, 1943
Lives in New York

ONE-ARTIST EXHIBITIONS

1974 Museum of Art, Carnegie Institute, Pittsburgh
1977 London Film Makers Co-op
1978 Pacific Film Archive, University Art Museum, University of California, Berkeley
1979 The Museum of Modern Art, New York
1980 Walker Art Center, Minneapolis
1981 Collective for Living Cinema, New York
1982 Musée National d'Art Moderne, Centre Georges Pompidou, Paris
1983 School of the Art Institute of Chicago
     Whitney Museum of American Art, New York
1985 Millennium, New York

GROUP EXHIBITIONS

1976 The American Federation of Arts, New York, "A History of the American Avant-Garde Cinema"
     Musée National d'Art Moderne, Centre Georges Pompidou, Paris, "Une Histoire du Cinéma"
1977 New York State Gallery Association, "Film as Art" (traveled)
1978 Media Study, Buffalo, "The Moving Image"
1981 Moderna Museet, Stockholm, "The Pleasure Dome"
     Whitney Museum of American Art, New York, "1981 Biennial Exhibition" (traveled)
1982 Lincoln Center for the Performing Arts, New York, "The Twentieth New York Film Festival"
1983 Whitney Museum of American Art, New York, "1983 Biennial Exhibition" (traveled)
1986 Turin, Italy, "The Turin Film Festival"

BIBLIOGRAPHY

Gunning, Thomas. "The Critique of Seeing with One's Own Eyes: Ernie Gehr's 'Untitled' (1976)." *Millennium Film Journal*, no. 12 (Fall-Winter 1982–83), pp. 134–36.

Hanhardt, John G. "Ernie Gehr" (program notes). *The New American Filmmakers Series* 9. New York: Whitney Museum of American Art, 1983.

Hoberman, J. "Ride On." *The Village Voice*, October 11, 1983, p. 52.

Mekas, Jonas. "Ernie Gehr Interviewed by Jonas Mekas, March 24, 1971." *Film Culture*, no. 53-54-55 (Spring 1972), pp. 25–36.

Sitney, P. Adams. *Visionary Film: The American Avant Garde, 1943–1978*. 2nd ed. New York: Oxford University Press, 1979, pp. 369, 373, 381, 436–40, 443.

PAUL GLABICKI

Born in Pittsburgh, 1951
Studied at Carnegie-Mellon University, Pittsburgh (B.F.A., 1972); Ohio University, Athens (M.F.A., 1974; M.F.A., 1979)
Lives in Pittsburgh

ONE-ARTIST EXHIBITIONS

1982 Ann Arbor Film Festival
     Berks Filmmakers, Reading, Pennsylvania
     Philadelphia College of Art
1984 School of the Art Institute of Chicago
1985 Museum of Art, Carnegie Institute, Pittsburgh
1986 Athens International Film Festival, Ohio
     Donnell Media Center, New York Public Library
     Virginia Museum of Fine Arts, Richmond

GROUP EXHIBITIONS

1978 Film Forum, New York, "New Directions in American Animation"
1979 Hirshhorn Museum and Sculpture Garden, Smithsonian Institution, Washington, D.C., "New American Animators"
1982 Film Forum, New York, "New Directions in American Animation"
1983 Northwest Film Study Center, Eugene, Oregon, "New American Animation"
1985 Hiroshima International Animation Festival of Japan
1986 The American Federation of Arts, New York, "Synthetic Movements"
     Image Forum, Tokyo, "New American Animation"
     Stuttgart Animation Festival

BIBLIOGRAPHY

Glabicki, Paul. *"Diagram Film."* In *Frames: Statements and Drawings by American Independent Animators*, edited by George Griffin. New York: Metropolis Graphics, 1978, unpaginated.

———. *Wipes* (Animators' Flip Book Collection), edited by George Griffin. New York: Metropolis Graphics, 1981.

Levine, Barry. "Redefinitions." In *Synthetic Movements: New Directions for Contemporary American Animation*. New York: The American Federation of Arts, 1981, pp. 10–11.

Martell, Maxine. "Paul Glabicki." In *Suspended Animation*. Seattle: and/or, 1979.

Millsapps, Jan. "Paul Glabicki: Formalism as a Way of Life." *Independent Spirit*, 4 (Winter 1983), pp. 5–7.

SHALOM GOREWITZ

Born in New York, 1949
Studied at Antioch College, Yellow Springs, Ohio (1967–70); California Institute of the Arts, Valencia (B.F.A., 1971); Antioch University, Yellow Springs, Ohio (M.F.A., 1986)
Lives in New York

ONE-ARTIST EXHIBITIONS

1979 The Museum of Modern Art, New York
1980 Anthology Film Archives, New York
     Media Study, Buffalo
1981 University of California, Los Angeles
1982 Boston Film/Video Foundation
     Contemporary Arts Center, New Orleans
1984 The Bronx Museum of the Arts, New York
1985 International House, Neighborhood Film Project, Philadelphia
     Asahi Shimbon Cultural Center, Tokyo
1986 Semaphore Gallery, New York

GROUP EXHIBITIONS

1979 The Kitchen, New York, "Image Processing"
1980 The Kitchen, New York, "Videotapes from the Kitchen Center for Video and Music" (traveled)
     San Francisco International Video Festival
1981 Genoa Arts Council, Italy, "The Restless Language"
     Whitney Museum of American Art, New York "1981 Biennial Exhibition"
1982 American Center, Paris, "Tapes from the Experimental Television Center"
1983 Whitney Museum of American Art, New York, "1983 Biennial Exhibition" (traveled)
1985 Alternative Museum, New York, "Collaborations"
1986 Il Festival Nacional Video, Madrid

BIBLIOGRAPHY

Ancona, Victor. "Video Art: Shalom Gorewitz, Metaphoric Image Manipulator." *Videography*, 5 (November 1980), pp. 62–67.

Gorewitz, Shalom. *Dissonant Landscapes*. Yellow Springs, Ohio: Antioch University, 1986.

_____. "Passages at the Experimental Television Center." *The Independent*, 6 (November 1983), pp. 19–21.
Wooster, Ann-Sargent. "Flicks and Tapes." *Art in America*, 69 (May 1981), pp. 123–28.

DAN GRAHAM

Born in Urbana, Illinois, 1942
Lives in New York

ONE-ARTIST EXHIBITIONS

1973 Galerie Rudolf Zwirner, Cologne
1974 Galerie 17, Paris
1975 Palais des Beaux-Arts, Brussels
1976 Sperone Westwater Fischer, New York
1977 Galerie René Block, West Berlin
1980 The Museum of Modern Art, New York
1982 Parachute, Montreal
1983 Kunsthalle Bern, Switzerland
1985 The Art Gallery of Western Australia, Perth
1986 Cable Gallery, New York

GROUP EXHIBITIONS

1970 The Museum of Modern Art, New York "Information"
1971 Museum of Fine Arts, Boston, "Earth, Air, Fire, Water: Elements of Art"
1972 Kassel, West Germany, "Documenta 5"
1975 Institute of Contemporary Art, University of Pennsylvania, Philadelphia, "Video Art"
1977 Musée National d'Art Moderne, Centre Georges Pompidou, Paris, "Opening Exhibition of the Permanent Collection"
1978 Leo Castelli Gallery, New York, "Numerals 1924–1977"
1982 Rüdiger Schöttle, Munich, "Godard, Barry, Graham, Knight"
1985 The Museum of Modern Art, New York, "New Video Acquisitions"
The New Museum of Contemporary Art, New York, "The Art of Memory/The Loss of History"
1986 Musée National d'Art Moderne, Centre Georges Pompidou, Paris, "Les Immateriaux"

BIBLIOGRAPHY

Buchloh, Benjamin, H.D. "Documenta 7: A Dictionary of Received Ideas." *October*, 22 (Fall 1982), pp. 105–26.
Graham, Dan. "Interior Space/Exterior Space: An Addition to a Conventional House." In *Video Art: An Anthology*, edited by Ira Schneider and Beryl Korot. New York: Harcourt, Brace, Jovanovich, 1976, pp. 60–61.
_____. "Signs." *Artforum*, 19 (April 1981), pp. 38–43.
Kozloff, Max. "Pygmalion Reversed." *Artforum*, 14 (November 1975), pp. 30–37.

Russell, John. "A Contemplative Chicago Show." *The New York Times*, July 29, 1979, p. 31.

BARBARA HAMMER

Born in Hollywood, 1939
Studied at the University of California, Los Angeles (B.A., 1961); California State University at San Francisco (M.A., 1963; M.A., 1975)
Lives in Olympia, Washington

ONE-ARTIST EXHIBITIONS

1981 San Jose Museum of Art, California
1984 Canyon Cinema, San Francisco Filmforum, Los Angeles
1985 Collective for Living Cinema, New York
Musée National d'Art Moderne, Centre Georges Pompidou, Paris
The Museum of Modern Art, New York
1986 Berlin Film Festival, West Berlin
The Film Center, School of the Art Institute of Chicago
Semana Internacional de Cine Autor, Málaga, Spain

GROUP EXHIBITIONS

1980 Ny Carlsberg Glyptoteket, Copenhagen, "International Women's Performance Art"
1983 Pacific Film Archive, University Art Museum, University of California, Berkeley, "New Films from Canyon"
1985 Archives du Film Expérimental d'Avignon, France, "Trois Temporelites Filmiques"
Franklin Furnace and the Metropolitan Transportation Authority, Art For Transit Program, New York, "Live from Underground"
Museum Moderner Kunst, Vienna, "Kunst mit Eigen-Sinn"
1986 Ann Arbor Film Festival
Festival International de Films de Femmes, Creteil, France
Image Forum Cinémathèque, Tokyo, "American New Generation Cinema" (traveled)
New York City Experimental Film and Video Festival
Randolph Street Gallery, Chicago, "Sexual Inclinations"

BIBLIOGRAPHY

Beauvais, Yann. "Interview de Barbara Hammer." *Spiral*, 6 (January 1986), pp. 33–38.
Dunsford, Cath. "Barbara Hammer Is Alive and Well and Coming to New Zealand." *Alternative Cinema*, Autumn-Winter 1984.
Hulser, Kathleen. *Images de Passage: Neuf Films Récent de Barbara Hammer* (exhibition brochure). Paris: Musée National d'Art Moderne, Centre Georges Pompidou, 1985.

Kaplan, Ann E. *Women and Film: Both Sides of the Camera*. New York: Methuen, 1983, pp. 88–89.
Zita, Jacquelyn. "Films of Barbara Hammer." *JumpCut*, 24/25 (March 1981), pp. 27–30.

GARY HILL

Born in Santa Monica, California, 1951
Lives in New York and Seattle

ONE-ARTIST EXHIBITIONS

1974 South Houston Gallery, New York
1976 Anthology Film Archives, New York
1979 Everson Museum of Art of Syracuse and Onondaga County, Syracuse, New York
The Kitchen, New York
1980 The Museum of Modern Art, New York
1981 and/or, Seattle
1982 Long Beach Museum of Art, California
1983 Whitney Museum of American Art, New York
American Center, Paris
1986 Whitney Museum of American Art, New York

GROUP EXHIBITIONS

1974 55 Mercer Street Gallery, New York, "Artists from Upstate New York, Invitational"
1977 Everson Museum of Art of Syracuse and Onondaga County, Syracuse, New York, "New Work in Abstract Video Imagery"
1979 The Museum of Modern Art, New York, "Projects: Video XXVIII"
1980 Video 80/San Francisco Video Festival
1983 The Hudson River Museum, Yonkers, New York, "Electronic Visions"
Palais des Beaux-Arts, Charleroi, Belgium, "Video Retrospectives et Perspectives"
Walter Phillips Gallery, Banff, Alberta, Canada, "The Second Link: Viewpoints on Video in the Eighties" (traveled)
University Art Museum, University of New Mexico, Albuquerque, "Video as Attitude"
1984 Venice, Italy, "XLI Biennale di Venezia"
1985 Whitney Museum of American Art, New York, "1985 Biennial Exhibition" (traveled)

BIBLIOGRAPHY

Furlong, Lucinda. "A Manner of Speaking: An Interview with Gary Hill." *Afterimage*, 10 (March 1983), pp. 9–16.
Hanhardt, John G. "Gary Hill" (program notes). *The New American Filmmakers Series* 30. New York: Whitney Museum of American Art, 1986.

_____. "Gary Hill: *Primarily Speaking*" (program notes). *The New American Filmmakers Series* 12. New York: Whitney Museum of American Art, 1983.

Larson, Kay. "Art Through a Screen Dimly." *New York*, September 12, 1983, pp. 86–87.

Quasha, George. "Notes on the Feedback Horizon." In *Glass Onion* (program notes). Barrytown, New York: Station Hill Press, 1980.

LEANDRO KATZ

Born in Buenos Aires, 1938
Studied at Universidad Nacional de Buenos Aires (B.F.A., 1960)
Lives in New York

ONE-ARTIST EXHIBITIONS

1972 Centro de Arte y Comunicación, Buenos Aires
1977 Millennium, New York
1978 The Museum of Modern Art, New York
1980 The Clocktower, Institute for Art and Urban Resources, New York
Collective for Living Cinema, New York
1982 P.S. 1, Institute for Art and Urban Resources, Long Island City, New York
Whitney Museum of American Art, New York
1985 Collective for Living Cinema, New York
C.E.P.A., Buffalo

GROUP EXHIBITIONS

1978 John Gibson Gallery, New York, "Structure"
1979 Edinburgh International Film Festival
John Gibson Gallery, New York, "Structure II"
Whitney Museum of American Art, New York, "Allen Coulter/Leandro Katz"
1980 The Clocktower, Institute for Art and Urban Resources, New York, "Film as Installation"
1981 Berlin Film Festival, West Berlin
1982 Festival du Nouveau Cinéma, Montreal
1984 Museum of Art, Rhode Island School of Design, Providence, "Abstract Attitudes" (traveled)
1986 Festival du Nouveau Cinéma, Montreal
Rotterdam Film Festival

BIBLIOGRAPHY

Castle, Ted. "Verbal Art Speaks Up." *Flash Art*, no. 100 (November 1980), pp. 27–30.
_____. "Review of Exhibitions: Leandro Katz at the Center for Inter-American Relations and the Rhode Island School of Design." *Art in America*, 72 (October 1984), pp. 197–98.

Lawson, Thomas. "Reviews: Leandro Katz." *Artforum*, 21 (October 1982), p. 66.
Lippard, Lucy. *Overlay*. New York: Pantheon Books, 1983, pp. 94–95.
Silverman, Kaja. "Splits: Changing the Fantasmic Scene." *Framework*, 20 (1983), pp. 27–36.

ERNEST MARRERO AND SUSAN KOUGUELL

ERNEST MARRERO

Born in Guatemala City, Guatemala, 1959
Studied at the State University of New York, College at Purchase (B.A., 1982); Independent Study Program, Whitney Museum of American Art, New York (1981–82)
Lives in New York

SUSAN KOUGUELL

Born in New York, 1957
Studied at the State University of New York, College at Purchase (B.A., 1980); Independent Study Program, Whitney Museum of American Art, New York (1981–82)
Lives in New York

TWO-ARTIST EXHIBITIONS

1985 Collective for Living Cinema, New York

GROUP EXHIBITIONS

1982 Collective for Living Cinema, New York, "New Filmmakers Showcase"
Hirshhorn Museum and Sculpture Garden, Smithsonian Institution, Washington, D.C., "Prizewinners from the Baltimore International Film Festival"
1983 Collective for Living Cinema, New York, "Text as Film"
Marburg International Film Festival, West Germany
The Museum of Modern Art, New York, "New Acquisitions"
1985 Thomas A. Edison Black Maria Film Festival, West Orange, New Jersey
Mannheim International Film Festival, West Germany
Musée National d'Art Moderne, Centre Georges Pompidou, Paris "Cinéma Expérimental Américain 1905–1984" (traveled)
1986 Collective for Living Cinema, New York

BIBLIOGRAPHY

Freedman, Richard. "Film Fest Takes Pioneering Path." *Newark Star Ledger*, November 19, 1982, p. 51.

NINA MENKES

Born in Ann Arbor, Michigan, 1955
Studied at the University of California, Berkeley (B.A., 1977); University of California, Los Angeles (1980–86)
Lives in Los Angeles

ONE-ARTIST EXHIBITIONS

1979 Robert H. Lowie Museum of Anthropology, University of California, Berkeley, California
1983 Streisand Center for Cultural Arts, Los Angeles

GROUP EXHIBITIONS

1984 Edinburgh International Film Festival
Houston International Film Festival
Mannheim International Film Festival, West Germany
San Francisco International Film Festival
1985 Torino, Italy, Festival Internationale de Cinema Giovanni
1986 Festival du Nouveau Cinéma, Montreal
Festival International de Films de Femmes, Creteil, France
Florence Film Festival
International Festival of Jewish Culture, Paris
Mannheim International Film Festival, West Germany

BIBLIOGRAPHY

Hofferman, Jon. "*Magdalena Viraga*: Story of a Red Sea Crossing." *Los Angeles Reader*, November 7, 1986, p. 13.
Rockman, Hadasah. "Film Search for the Spiritual." *The Jerusalem Post*, August 24, 1986, p. 5.
Thomas, Kevin. "Poetry and Passion in *Magdalena*." *Los Angeles Times*, November 10, 1986, p. 2.

SHERRY MILLNER

Born in Brooklyn, New York, 1950
Studied at the California Institute of the Arts, Valencia (B.A., 1976); University of California, San Diego (M.F.A., 1982)
Lives in New York

ONE-ARTIST EXHIBITIONS

1982 Sushi Gallery, San Diego
1983 Pasadena Filmforum, California
1984 Center for Art Tapes, Halifax, Nova Scotia
San Francisco Cinémathèque
Walker Art Center, Minneapolis
1986 Los Angeles Center for Photographic Studies

GROUP EXHIBITIONS

1984 Collective for Living Cinema, New York, "Sherry Millner and Jeffrey Skoller"

American Film Institute, National Video
Festival Olympic Screenings, Los
Angeles and Washington, D.C.,
"Thinking Television: Low-Tech
Representations"
Walker Art Center, Minneapolis, "Stories
of Her Own"
1985 American Film Institute, Washington,
D.C. and Los Angeles, "National Video
Festival"
Long Beach Museum of Art, California,
"Open Channels"
1986 American Museum of the Moving
Image, New York, "California Video"
Minneapolis College of Art and Design,
"Life Stories"
Women's Building, Los Angeles,
"Women Make Videos"

BIBLIOGRAPHY

DeMichiel, Helen. "Speculations: Narrative
Video by Women." *The Independent*, 8
(April 1985), pp. 12–14.
Kruger, Barbara. "Reviews: Sherry Millner,
'Crime Around the Collar,' the Collective
for Living Cinema." *Artforum*, 22 (March
1984), pp. 91–92.
Lord, Catherine. "Thinking Television:
Low-Tech Representations." In *National
Video Festival Olympic Screenings*
(exhibition catalogue). Los Angeles and
Washington, D.C.: American Film
Institute, 1984.
McGee, Micki. "Public Art." *Fuse*, 10
(March 1982) pp. 303–05.
Millner, Sherry. "Third World Newsreel:
Interview with Christine Choy." *JumpCut*,
27 (July 1982), pp. 21–23. Reprinted in
*JumpCut: Hollywood Politics and Counter
Cinema*, edited by Peter Steven. Toronto:
Between the Lines, 1985.

YVONNE RAINER

Born in San Francisco, 1934
Lives in New York

ONE-ARTIST EXHIBITIONS

1974 Whitney Museum of American Art,
New York
1975 The Museum of Modern Art,
New York
1977 The Other Cinema, London
1981 Academy of Motion Picture Arts and
Sciences, Los Angeles
Bleecker Street Cinema, New York
1982 American Film Institute, Los Angeles
1985 University of California, Santa Cruz
Walker Art Center, Minneapolis
1986 Bleecker Street Cinema, New York
Whitney Museum of American Art,
New York

GROUP EXHIBITIONS

1974 Cannes Film Festival
Kölnischer Kunstverein, Cologne,
"Projekt '74"

Montreux, Switzerland, "New Forms in
Film"
1975 Edinburgh International Film Festival
1977 Berlin Film Festival, West Berlin
1980 The Kitchen, New York,
"Filmworks '80"
Rotterdam Film Festival
1981 Whitney Museum of American Art,
New York, "1981 Biennial Exhibition"
(traveled)
1985 Montreal Women's Film Festival

BIBLIOGRAPHY

Carroll, Noel. "Interview with a Woman
Who . . . ." *Millennium Film Journal*, no.
7/8/9 (Fall-Winter 1980–1981), pp. 37–68.
Kaplan, E. Ann. *Women and Film*. New
York: Methuen, 1983.
Kuhn, Annette. *Women's Pictures*. London:
Routledge and Kegan Paul, 1982.
Rainer, Yvonne. "Some Ruminations
Around Cinematic Antidotes to the
Oedipal Net[les] While Playing with
De Lauraedipus Mulvey, or He May Be
Off Screen, But . . . ." *The Independent*, 9
(April 1986), pp. 22–25.
Storr, Robert. "The Theoretical Come-On."
Art in America, 74 (April 1986),
pp. 158–65.

RACHEL REICHMAN

Born in St. Louis, 1958
Studied at the School of Visual Arts, New
York (B.F.A., 1980)
Lives in New York

ONE-ARTIST EXHIBITIONS

1986 The Kitchen, New York

GROUP EXHIBITIONS

1986 Chicago International Film Festival
Festival du Nouveau Cinéma, Montreal
Florence Film Festival
Independent Feature Market, New York
Munich Film Festival
Rotterdam Film Festival

BIBLIOGRAPHY

Baxter, Brian. "Brussels and Rotterdam:
Two Festivals Different in Concept and
Intention." *Films and Filming*, April 1986,
p. 26.
Wall. "The Riverbed." *Variety*, February 19,
1986, p. 291.

MARTHA ROSLER

Born in New York, 1943
Studied at Brooklyn College, New York
(B.A., 1965); University of California,
San Diego (M.F.A., 1974)
Lives in New York

ONE-ARTIST EXHIBITIONS

1977 Long Beach Museum of Art,
California
Whitney Museum of American Art,
New York
1978 and/or, Seattle
Video Free America, San Francisco
1979 A Space, Toronto
University Art Museum, University of
California, Berkeley
1981 Franklin Furnace, New York
1982 Dance Theater Workshop, New York
1986 Electronic Arts Gallery, Minneapolis
Installation Gallery, San Diego

GROUP EXHIBITIONS

1979 Whitney Museum of American Art,
New York, "1979 Biennial Exhibition"
1980 Institute of Contemporary Arts,
London, "Issue!"
1982 The Biennale of Sydney, Australia
Kassel, West Germany, "Documenta 7"
1983 Institute of Contemporary Art,
Boston, "Video of the Seventies—The
Greatest Hits" (traveled)
Whitney Museum of American Art, New
York, "1983 Biennial Exhibition"
(traveled)
1984 Hirshhorn Museum and Sculpture
Garden, Smithsonian Institution,
Washington, D.C., "Content: A
Contemporary Focus"
The New Museum of Contemporary Art,
New York, "Difference: On
Representation and Sexuality" (traveled)
1985 Film in the Cities, St. Paul,
"ArtSide Out"
The New Museum of Contemporary Art,
New York, "The Art of Memory/The
Loss of History"

BIBLIOGRAPHY

Buchloh, Benjamin H.D. "From Gadget
Video to Agit Video: Some Notes on
Four Recent Video Works." *Art Journal*,
45 (Fall 1985), pp. 217–28.
Owens, Craig. "Martha Rosler"
(interview). Chicago: Profile Series,
Video Data Bank, 1986.
Rosler, Martha. "Lookers, Buyers, Dealers,
and Makers: Thoughts on the Audience."
Exposure, 1 (Spring 1979), pp. 10–25.
Reprinted in *Art After Modernism:
Rethinking Representation*, edited by Brian
Wallis. New York and Boston: The New
Museum of Contemporary Art and David
Godine, 1985, pp. 311–39.
———. *Martha Rosler, Three Works*. Halifax,
Nova Scotia: The Press of the Nova
Scotia College of Art and Design, 1981.
———. "Video: Shedding the Utopian
Moment." In *Vidéo*, edited by René
Payant. Montreal: Artexte, 1986,
pp. 242-51.

MATTHEW SCHLANGER

Born in Brooklyn, New York, 1958
Studied at the State University of New York at Binghamton (B.A., 1981)
Lives in Brooklyn, New York

ONE-ARTIST EXHIBITIONS

1984 Millennium, New York
Boston Film/Video Foundation

GROUP EXHIBITIONS

1981 The Kitchen, New York, "Experimental Television Workshop Benefit"
1982 The Kitchen, New York, "Image/Process"
1983 The Leonard Davis Center for Performing Arts, City College of New York, "Artist and Computer"
1984 Global Village, New York, "Romance and Mystery"
P.S. 1, Institute for Art and Urban Resources, Long Island City, New York, "Abstraction and Image Processing"
WNYC-TV, New York, "Videoville"
1985 The Bronx Museum of the Arts, New York, "Emerging Expression: The Artist and Computer"
The Kitchen, New York, "Experimental Television Workshop Anthology"
Limbo Lounge, New York, "Techno-Bop"
1986 The New Museum of Contemporary Art, New York, "Views"

BIBLIOGRAPHY

Archer, Chris. "Festival Shows Breaking of Barriers Between Film, Video." *The Villager*, May 16, 1985, p. 11.
Connolly, Marc. "BACA Scores a Hit with Film/Video Festival." *Phoenix*, May 16, 1985, p. 14.

WARREN SONBERT

Born in New York, 1947
Studied at New York University (B.A., 1969)
Lives in San Francisco

ONE-ARTIST EXHIBITIONS

1971 The Museum of Modern Art, New York
1976 Österreichisches Filmmuseum, Vienna
Whitney Museum of American Art, New York
1977 School of the Art Institute of Chicago
1980 The Museum of Modern Art, New York
1982 Münchner Stadtmuseum, Munich
1983 Pacific Film Archive, University Art Museum, University of California, Berkeley
1985 Cinémaprodif, Paris
1986 Bela Balasz Studios, Budapest
Deutsches Filmmuseum, Frankfurt

GROUP EXHIBITIONS

1970 National Film Archive, London, "First International Experimental Film Festival"
1974 Los Angeles Film Exposition
1975 Musée National d'Art Moderne, Centre Georges Pompidou, Paris, "First International Film Exhibition"
1977 Berlin Film Festival, West Berlin
1979 Whitney Museum of American Art, New York, "1979 Biennial Exhibition" (traveled)
1980 Mill Valley Film Festival, Mill Valley, California
Moderna Museet, Stockholm, "New American Cinema"
1983 Whitney Museum of American Art, New York, "1983 Biennial Exhibition" (traveled)
1984 The Kitchen, New York, "Best Films of the Year"
1985 Whitney Museum of American Art, New York, "1985 Biennial Exhibition" (traveled)

BIBLIOGRAPHY

Carroll, Noel. "Causation, the Ampliation of Movement and Avant-Garde Film." *Millennium Film Journal*, no. 10/11 (Fall-Winter 1981–82), pp. 61–82.
Hanhardt, John G. "Warren Sonbert" (program notes). *The New American Filmmakers Series* 10. New York: Whitney Museum of American Art, 1983.
Sitney, P. Adams. "Point of View: Rear-Garde." *American Film*, 10 (July-August 1985), pp. 13, 61.
Sonbert, Warren. "Cappriccio, Part I." *Motion Picture*, 1 (Spring-Summer 1986), pp. 4, 18.
———. "Narrative Concerns." *Poetics Journal*, no. 5 (May 1985), pp. 107–10.

SKIP SWEENEY

Born in San Mateo, California, 1946
Studied at the University of Santa Clara, California (B.A., 1968)
Lives in San Francisco

ONE-ARTIST EXHIBITIONS

1970 Intersection Theater, San Francisco
1975 WNET-TV, New York
1976 Anthology Film Archives, New York
1983 Institute of Contemporary Art, Boston
The Museum of Modern Art, New York
1984 The Exploratorium, San Francisco
1986 Pacific Film Archive, University Art Museum, University of California, Berkeley

GROUP EXHIBITIONS

1971 Brooklyn Academy of Music, New York
Pacific Film Archive, University Art Museum, University of California, Berkeley

1977 Everson Museum of Art of Syracuse and Onondaga County, Syracuse, New York
1983 American Film Institute, Los Angeles and Washington, D.C., "National Video Festival"
1984 Video Culture Canada, Toronto
1985 The Museum of Modern Art, New York. "TV Lab Retrospective"
Washington Project for the Arts Gallery, Washington, D.C.
1986 Global Village, New York, "Global Village Documentary Film Festival"
The Kitchen, New York

BIBLIOGRAPHY

Ancona, Victor. "Skip Sweeney: Video as a Redemptive Medium." *Videography*, 8 (August 1983), pp. 72–78.
Klein, Sami. "Everybody Will Be on Television." *Rolling Stone*, March 18, 1971, pp. 22–23.
Mekas, Jonas. "Movie Journal." *The Village Voice*, December 2, 1971.
O'Connor, John J. "PBS Offers My Mother Married Wilbur Stump." *The New York Times*, May 9, 1986, p. C26.

TRINH T. MINH-HA

Born in Hanoi, 1952
Studied at the Sorbonne, Paris (1974–75); University of Illinois, Urbana-Champaign (M.A., 1973; M.A., 1976; Ph.D., 1977)
Lives in Berkeley, California

ONE-ARTIST EXHIBITIONS

1983 Film in the Cities, St. Paul, Minnesota
UNESCO, Dakar, Senegal
1984 Teatro la Maddelena, Rome
1985 National Film Theater, London
1986 Artists Space, New York
Commonwealth Institute Arts Centre, London
Robert Flaherty Film Seminar, Wells College, Aurora, New York
Stanford University, Palo Alto, California
Whitney Museum of American Art, New York

GROUP EXHIBITIONS

1983 American Film Institute, Los Angeles, "Women and Movies III"
Festival dei Popoli, Florence
Lincoln Center for the Performing Arts, New York, "Twenty-first New York Film Festival"
1984 Atlanta Third World Film Festival
Hong Kong International Film Festival
1985 Toronto Film Festival
1986 Edinburgh International Film Festival, "Third World Cinema: Theories and Practices"
Festival de Films et Videos de Femmes, Montreal

Festival International de Films de
Femmes, Creteil, France
International Women's Film Festival of
Jerusalem

BIBLIOGRAPHY

Furlong, Lucinda. "Images of Culture: The
Films of Trinh T. Minh-ha" (program
notes). *The New American Filmmakers
Series* 32. New York: Whitney Museum of
American Art, 1986.
Penley, Constance, and Andrew Ross.
"Interview with Trinh T. Minh-ha."
Camera Obscura, 13–14 (Spring-Summer
1985), pp. 87–111.
Trinh, Minh-ha T. *Un Art sans Oeuvre*. Troy,
Michigan: International Book Publishers,
1981.
———. "Mechanical Eye, Electronic Ear
and the Lure of Authenticity." *Wide
Angle*, 6 (Summer 1984), pp. 58–63.
———, and Jean-Paul Bourdier. *African
Spaces: Designs for Living in Upper Volta*.
London and New York: Holmes and
Meier, 1985.

BILL VIOLA

Born in New York, 1951
Studied at Syracuse University, New York
(B.F.A., 1973)
Lives in Long Beach, California

ONE-ARTIST EXHIBITIONS

1975 Everson Museum of Art of Syracuse
and Onondaga County, Syracuse,
New York
1977 The Kitchen, New York
1979 The Museum of Modern Art,
New York
1980 Long Beach Museum of Art,
California
1981 Vancouver Art Gallery, British
Columbia
1982 Seibu Museum of Art, Tokyo
Whitney Museum of American Art,
New York
1983 Musée d'Art Moderne de la Ville de
Paris
1985 Moderna Museet, Stockholm
San Francisco Museum of Modern Art

GROUP EXHIBITIONS

1974 Kölnischer Kunstverein, Cologne,
"Projekt '74"
1977 Kassel, West Germany, "Documenta 6"
1980 The Museum of Modern Art, New
York, "Projects: Video"
1982 The Biennale of Sydney, Australia
1983 Museum of Fine Arts, Santa Fe, New
Mexico, "Video as Attitude"
1984 Long Beach Museum of Art,
California, "California Video 1984"
Stedelijk Museum, Amsterdam, "The
Luminous Image"

1985 The Museum of Contemporary Art,
Los Angeles, "Summer 1985"
Whitney Museum of American Art, New
York, "1985 Biennial Exhibition"
1986 Venice, Italy, "XLII Biennale di
Venezia"

BIBLIOGRAPHY

Bellour, Raymond. "An Interview with
Bill Viola." *October*, 34 (Fall 1985),
pp. 91–119.
Hoberman, J. "The Island Earth." *The
Village Voice*, September 30, 1986, p. 61.
Minkowsky, John. "Bill Viola's Video
Visions." *Video 80*, Fall 1981, pp. 32–34.
Sturken, Marita. "Temporal Interventions:
The Videotapes of Bill Viola." *Afterimage*,
10 (Summer 1982), pp. 28–31.
Viola, Bill. "Bill Viola, Statements by the
Artist." In *Summer 1985* (exhibition
catalogue). Los Angeles: The Museum of
Contemporary Art, 1985.

BRUCE YONEMOTO
AND NORMAN YONEMOTO

BRUCE YONEMOTO

Born in San Jose, California, 1949
University of California, Berkeley (B.A.,
1972); Sokei Art Institute, Tokyo (1973–
75); Otis Art Institute, Los Angeles
(M.F.A., 1979)
Lives in Venice, California

NORMAN YONEMOTO

Born in Chicago, 1946
Studied at the University of Santa Clara,
California (1965–67); University of
California, Berkeley (1967–68);
University of California, Los Angeles
(1968–70); American Film Institute
Center for Advanced Film Studies, Los
Angeles (1972–73)
Lives in Santa Monica, California

TWO-ARTIST EXHIBITIONS

1980 University Art Museum, University of
California, Berkeley
1982 Franklin Furnace, New York
Long Beach Museum of Art, California
Los Angeles Contemporary Exhibitions
1984 Anthology Film Archives, New York
Image Forum, Tokyo
The Museum of Contemporary Art, Los
Angeles
1985 American Film Institute, Los Angeles
Hallwalls, Buffalo
1986 Baskerville + Watson, New York

GROUP EXHIBITIONS

1980 11me Biennal de Paris, "California
Video" (traveled)

Long Beach Museum of Art, California,
"N/A Vision" (traveled)
1983 Institute of Contemporary Art,
Boston, "The New Soap"
Video Data Bank, Chicago, "Chicago Art
Exhibition"
1984 Kijkhuis, The Hague, "World-Wide
Video Festival"
The Museum of Modern Art, New York,
"New Narrative: Recent Video
Acquisitions"
1985 The Museum of Modern Art, New
York, "Video from Vancouver to San
Diego"
Whitney Museum of American Art, New
York, "1985 Biennial Exhibition"
(traveled)
1986 Channel 4, Great Britain, "Ghosts in
the Machine"
PBS, KTCA/TV, Twin Cities Public
Television, Minneapolis/St. Paul, "Alive
from Off Center"

BIBLIOGRAPHY

Houston, Beverle. "Television and Video
Text: A Crisis of Desire." In *Resolution: A
Critique of Video Art*. Los Angeles: Los
Angeles Contemporary Exhibitions, 1986,
pp. 110–24.
James, David. "Questioning the Signifiers."
Artweek, September 11, 1982, p. 5.
Pincus, Robert L. "Video Art that
Deconstructs." *Los Angeles Times*,
June 10, 1984, p. 100.
Podheiser, Linda. *Revising Romance: New
Feminist Video* (exhibition catalogue).
New York: The American Federation of
Arts, with the cooperation of the
Institute of Contemporary Art, Boston,
1984.
Sturken, Marita. "Feminist Video:
Reiterating the Difference." *Afterimage*, 9
(April 1985), pp. 9–11.

Dimensions are in inches, followed by centimeters;
height precedes width precedes depth.

PAINTING SCULPTURE PHOTOGRAPHY

RICHARD ARTSCHWAGER

Dinner (Two), 1986
Acrylic on Celotex with painted wood
    frame, 27¾ x 55¾ (70.5 x 141.6)
Private collection

*The Organ of Cause
    and Effect III*, 1986
Formica and acrylic on wood, 129 x 61¾ x
    18 (327.7 x 156.8 x 45.7)
Donald Young Gallery, Chicago

Two Diners, 1987
Acrylic on Celotex and formica with
    painted wood frame, 91¾ x 79¼
    (233.6 x 200.7)
Leo Castelli Gallery, New York

TINA BARNEY

The Reception, 1985
Color photograph, Ektachrome print,
    48 x 60 (121.9 x 152.4)
Janet Borden, Inc., New York

The Birthday Cake, 1986
Color photograph, Ektachrome print,
    48 x 60 (121.9 x 152.4)
Janet Borden, Inc., New York

The Card Party, 1986
Color photograph, Ektachrome print,
    48 x 60 (121.9 x 152.4)
Janet Borden, Inc., New York

JUDITH BARRY

First and Third, 1986
Video installation: video projector
    and videotape
Collection of the artist

DAVID BATES

Kingfisher, 1985
Oil on canvas, 96 x 78 (243.8 x 198.1)
Collection of Laila and Thurston
    Twigg-Smith

Catfish Moon, 1986
Oil on canvas, 84 x 64 (213.4 x 162.6)
Collection of Lucy Norsworthy

Red Moon, 1986
Oil on canvas, 84 x 64 (213.4 x 162.6)
Collection of Mr. and Mrs. John Strauss

ROSS BLECKNER

The Oceans, 1984–86
Oil and wax on canvas, 120 x 144
    (304.8 x 365.8)
Collection of Jerry and Emily Spiegel

Untitled, 1985
Oil on linen, 96 x 72 (243.8 x 182.9)
Collection of Julian Schnabel

Twelve Nights, 1986
Oil on canvas, 76 x 62 (193 x 157.5)
Mary Boone Gallery, New York

LOUISE BOURGEOIS

Legs, 1986
Rubber; two pieces, each 123 x 2 x 2
    (312.4 x 5.1 x 5.1)
Robert Miller Gallery, New York

Nature Study, 1986
Marble, 33 x 28 x 21½ (83.8 x 71.1 x 54.6)
Private collection

Nature Study, 1986
Marble, 35 x 61 x 29 (88.9 x 154.9 x 73.7)
Robert Miller Gallery, New York

JOHN CHAMBERLAIN

First Dance of the Trees, 1986
Painted steel and chromium-plated steel,
    84 x 108 x 60 (213.4 x 274.3 x 152.4)
Xavier Fourcade, Inc., New York

Iceberg, 1986
Painted steel and chromium-plated steel,
    84 x 65 x 40 (213.4 x 165.1 x 101.6)
Xavier Fourcade, Inc., New York

CLEGG & GUTTMANN

Corporate Music, 1985
Color photograph, Cibachrome print,
    laminated to plexiglass, 72 x 96
    (182.9 x 243.8)
Cable Gallery, New York

The Financiers, 1986
Color photograph, Cibachrome print,
    laminated to plexiglass, 75 x 96
    (190.5 x 243.8)
Jay Gorney Modern Art, New York

The Gallery Proprietesses, 1986
Color photograph, Cibachrome print,
    laminated to plexiglass, 67 x 81
    (170.2 x 205.7)
Cable Gallery, New York

GEORGE CONDO

Dancing to Miles, 1985–86
Oil on canvas, 110¼ x 137¾ (280 x 349.9)
Collection of the Eli Broad Family
    Foundation

Black Insect, 1986
Oil on canvas, 78¾ x 78¾ (200 x 200)
Larry Gagosian Gallery, Los Angeles

Girl with the Purple Dress, 1986
Oil on canvas, 78¾ x 70¾ (200 x 179.7)
Collection of Asher Edelman

WILLEM DE KOONING

Untitled XII, 1986
Oil on canvas, 70 x 80 (177.8 x 203.2)
Xavier Fourcade, Inc., New York

Untitled XVIII, 1986
Oil on canvas, 70 x 80 (177.8 x 203.2)
Xavier Fourcade, Inc., New York

NANCY DWYER

Coming Up Next, 1986
Acrylic on canvas, 60 x 75 (152.4 x 190.5)
Collection of Joel Wachs

Human, 1986
Formica on wood, 60 x 60 x 22
    (152.4 x 152.4 x 55.9)
Josh Baer Gallery, New York

Your Name, 1986
Enamel on plexiglass, formica on wood,
    and electric lights, 37 x 47 x 5
    (94 x 119.4 x 12.7)
Collection of Fried, Frank, Harris and
    Shriver, Inc.

R.M. FISCHER

Northstar, 1986
Aluminum, brass, and electric lights,
104¼ x 54½ x 18 (264.8 x 138.4 x 45.7)
Collection of Lynne and Ernie Meiger

Snap, Crackle, Pop, 1986
Aluminum, chrome-plated steel, stainless
steel, brass, plastic, and electric lights,
89 x 114 x 36 (226.1 x 289.6 x 91.4)
Collection of the Eli Broad Family
Foundation

LOUISE FISHMAN

Refiner's Fire, 1985
Oil on linen, 32 x 19¼ (81.3 x 48.9)
Winston Gallery, Washington, D.C.

Ida's Special, 1986
Oil on linen, 61¼ x 36½ (155.6 x 92.7)
Collection of John Sacchi

Smuggler's Notch, 1986
Oil on linen, 24 x 16 (61 x 40.6)
Collection of Edward R. Downe, Jr.

ROBERT GREENE

The Wedding, 1985
Oil on board, 42 x 54 (106.7 x 137.2)
Private collection

Another Always, 1986
Oil on canvas, 82 x 48 (208.3 x 121.9)
Robert Miller Gallery, New York

Private Thoughts, 1986
Oil on board, 45 x 62 (114.3 x 157.5)
Collection of the artist

PETER HALLEY

Two Cells with Circulating Conduit, 1985
Acrylic and Roll-A-Tex on canvas, 64 x 108
(162.6 x 274.3)
Collection of Susan and Richard Katcher

Blue Cell with Triple Conduit, 1986
Acrylic and Roll-A-Tex on canvas, 77 x 77
(195.6 x 195.6)
Collection of Robert and Adrian Mnuchin

Three Sectors, 1986
Acrylic on canvas, 58 x 192 (147.3 x 487.7)
Collection of The Interpublic Group of
Companies, Inc.

ROBERT HELM

Falling Hour, 1986
Oil on wood with wood inlay and wood
frame, 23¾ x 30½ (60.3 x 77.5)
Neuberger Museum, State University of
New York at Purchase; Museum purchase
with funds made available from the
Awards in the Visual Arts Program with
assistance from the Roy R. Neuberger
Endowment Fund

Night Window, 1986
Oil on wood with wood inlay and wood
frame, 39¼ x 63¼ (99.7 x 160.7)
Private collection

Word by Word, 1986
Oil on wood with wood inlay and wood
frame, 31¼ x 63¼ (79.4 x 160.7)
Edward Thorp Gallery, New York

NEIL JENNEY

Atmosphere, 1975–85
Oil on wood with painted wood frame,
33 x 79½ x 5¼ (83.8 x 200.7 x 13.3)
Collection of Mr. and Mrs. Keith L. Sachs

Venus from North America, 1979–87
Oil on wood with painted wood frame,
85 x 53¼ x 3⅛ (215.9 x 135.1 x 7.9)
Collection of the artist

ROBERTO JUAREZ

Applepeppers, 1986
Acrylic and collage on burlap, 72 x 72
(182.9 x 182.9)
Collection of Bruce Camay and
John Stimmel

Lima, 1986
Acrylic and collage on burlap, 73 x 73
(185.4 x 185.4)
Collection of Ena Swansea

Off-Shore Drilling, 1986
Acrylic and collage on canvas, 73 x 73
(185.4 x 185.4)
Private collection, courtesy Robert Miller
Gallery, New York

JEFF KOONS

One Ball Total Equilibrium Tank, 1985
Glass, iron, water, and basketball,
64¾ x 30¾ x 13¼ (164.5 x 78.1 x 33.7)
Collection of Michael H. Schwartz

Two Ball 50-50 Tank, 1985
Glass, iron, water, and basketballs,
62¾ x 36¾ x 13¼ (159.4 x 93.3 x 33.7)
Collection of Susan and Lewis Manilow

Rabbit, 1986
Stainless steel, 41 x 19 x 12
(104.1 x 48.3 x 30.5)
Private collection, courtesy Sonnabend
Gallery, New York

JOSEPH KOSUTH

Word, Sentence, Paragraph (Z. & N.),
1986
Photo-offset printing on paper, and neon,
72¼ x 90 (183.5 x 228.6)
Collection of Raymond J. Learsy

Zero & Not, 1986
Photo-offset printing on paper,
dimensions variable
Leo Castelli Gallery, New York

BARBARA KRUGER

Untitled (I Shop Therefore I Am), 1987
Photographic silkscreen on vinyl, 120 x 120
(304.8 x 304.8)
Collection of the artist, courtesy
Mary Boone Gallery, New York

*Untitled (In Space No One Can Hear
You Scream)*, 1987
Photographic silkscreen on vinyl,
120 x 204 (304.8 x 518.2)
Collection of the artist, courtesy
Mary Boone Gallery, New York

Untitled (Worth Every Penny), 1987
Photographic silkscreen on vinyl, 144 x 60
(365.8 x 152.4)
Collection of the artist, courtesy of Mary
Boone Gallery, New York

ANNETTE LEMIEUX

Homecoming, 1985
Oil on canvas with framed photograph
and framed book cover, 79 x 55
(200.7 x 139.7)
Collection of Michel Tournadre

Curious Child, 1986
Oil on canvas, 66 x 66 (167.6 x 167.6)
Cash/Newhouse Gallery, New York

Showing One's Colors, 1986
Oil on glass; three pieces, each 22 x 16½
(55.9 x 41.9)
Collection of Garry Webber

SOL LeWITT

Wall Drawing, 1987
Colored inks on wall
John Weber Gallery, New York

ROBERT LOBE

Killer Hill C.W., 1985
Aluminum, 99 x 184 x 27
(251.5 x 467.4 x 68.6)
Walker Art Center, Minneapolis;
Justin Smith Purchase Fund, 1986

Facial Structure, 1986
Aluminum, 120 x 144 x 114 (304.8 x
365.8 x 289.6)
Willard Gallery, New York

JIM LUTES

The Dry Waller, 1985
Oil on board, 56¾ x 34½ (144.1 x 87.6)
Private collection

The Evening of My Disfunction, 1985
Oil on canvas, 55 x 41½ (139.7 x 105.4)
Dart Gallery, Chicago

Field Day, 1986
Oil on canvas, 52 x 29 (132.1 x 73.7)
Dart Gallery, Chicago

DAVID McDERMOTT AND
PETER McGOUGH

The Big Show, 1928, 1986
Oil on linen with painted wood frame, light
    bulbs, and cord, 75 x 75 (190.5 x 190.5)
Collection of Diego Cortez

A Friend of Dorothy, 1943, 1986
Oil on canvas, 96 x 72 (243.8 x 182.9)
Collection of Robert and Jane Rosenblum

*Rub-a-Dub-Dub . . . Three Boys . . .
    and One Tub, 1937*, 1986
Oil on linen with painted wood frame,
    74½ x 74½ (189.2 x 189.2)
Collection of the Eli Broad Family
    Foundation

STEPHEN MUELLER

Radio Monaco, 1986
Acrylic on canvas, 90 x 70 (228.6 x 177.8)
Annina Nosei Gallery, New York

Rushing Up Portofino, 1986
Acrylic on canvas, 74 x 74 (188 x 188)
Annina Nosei Gallery, New York

St. George Lycabettus, 1986
Acrylic on canvas, 74 x 74 (188 x 188)
Collection of the artist

BRUCE NAUMAN

The Krefeld Piece, 1985
Video installation: videotape (*Good Boy/Bad
    Boy*), audiotape, and neon (*Hanged Man*)
Leo Castelli Gallery, New York

NAM JUNE PAIK

Family of Robot: Grandfather, 1986
Television cabinets, radio cabinet, color
    television sets, and videotape,
    101 x 73 x 20½ (256.5 x 185.4 x 52.1)
Collection of the artist, courtesy
    Holly Solomon Gallery, New York,
    and Carl Solway Gallery, Cincinnati

Family of Robot: Grandmother, 1986
Television cabinets, radio cabinet, color
    television sets, and videotape,
    80¾ x 50 x 19 (205.1 x 127 x 48.3)
Collection of the artist, courtesy
    Holly Solomon Gallery, New York,
    and Carl Solway Gallery, Cincinnati

IZHAR PATKIN

*The Black Paintings: Dawn, Black
    Rolls, Night, White Ghost*, 1985–86
Ink on neoprene; *Dawn* and *Night*, each
    14½ x 22 feet (44.2 x 67.1 meters); *Black
    Rolls* and *White Ghost*, each 14½ x 28 feet
    (44.2 x 85.3 meters)
Collection of the artist, courtesy Holly
    Solomon Gallery, New York

JUDY PFAFF

Untitled, 1987
Mixed-media installation,
    dimensions variable
Holly Solomon Gallery, New York

Untitled, 1987
Mixed-media installation,
    dimensions variable
Holly Solomon Gallery, New York

Illustrated (not in exhibition):
Supermercado, 1986
Painted wood and metal, 100½ x 163¾ x
    50 (255.3 x 127 x 415.9)
Whitney Museum of American Art, New
    York; Purchase, with funds from the
    Louis and Bessie Adler Foundation, Inc.,
    Seymour M. Klein, President; and the
    Sondra and Charles Gilman, Jr. Founda-
    tion, Inc.   86.34a–y
Wasco, 1986
Painted wood and metal, 77 x 148 x 48
    (195.6 x 375.9 x 121.9)
Holly Solomon Gallery, New York

LARI PITTMAN

An American Place, 1986
Acrylic and oil on wood, 80 x 164
    (203.2 x 416.6)
The Museum of Contemporary Art,
    Los Angeles; The El Paso Natural Gas
    Company Fund for California Art

Out of the Frost, 1986
Acrylic and oil on wood, 82 x 80
    (208.3 x 203.2)
Museum of Art, Carnegie Institute, Pitts-
    burgh; Gift of Tilly and Alexander C.
    Speyer Foundation Fund for the purchase
    of contemporary art

Reason to Rebuild, 1986
Acrylic and oil on wood, 82 x 80
    (208.3 x 203.2)
Collection of Douglas S. Cramer

RICHARD PRINCE

Live Free or Die, 1986
Color photograph, Ektachrome print,
    86 x 47 (218.4 x 119.4)
Collection of Arthur and Carol Goldberg

Tell Me Everything, 1986
Color photograph, Ektachrome print,
    86 x 47 (218.4 x 119.4)
Collection of Marvin and Alice Kosmin

Untitled (Joke), 1986
Color photograph, Ektachrome print,
    86 x 47 (218.4 x 119.4)
Private collection, courtesy International
    With Monument Gallery, New York

EDWARD RUSCHA

Name, Address, Phone, 1986
Acrylic on canvas, 59 x 145½
    (149.9 x 369.6)
Collection of Vance and Helen Lorenzini

The Uncertain Trail, 1986
Acrylic on canvas, 47 x 120 (119.4 x 304.8)
Leo Castelli Gallery, New York

ROBERT RYMAN

Century, 1985
Oil on aluminum, 49 x 45 (124.5 x 114.3)
Collection of Faith G. Golding

Charter, 1985
Oil on aluminum, 82 x 31 x 2½
    (208.3 x 78.7 x 6.4)
Collection of Gerald S. Elliott

Reference, 1985
Oil and enamelac on fiberglass, 102 x 38
    (259.1 x 96.5)
Collection of Thomas Ammann

ALAN SARET

Alchemicomania, 1986
Metal wire, 98 x 72 x 110
    (248.9 x 182.9 x 279.4)
Collection of the artist

Chosen Women, 1986
Metal wire; two pieces, 80 x 65 x 65
    (203.2 x 165.1 x 165.1) and 60 x 37 x 46
    (152.4 x 94 x 116.8)
Collection of the artist

JULIAN SCHNABEL

Mimi, 1986
Oil and linoleum on canvas with steer
    horns, 143 x 107½ (363.2 x 273.1)
Collection of Michael and Judy Ovitz

Virtue, 1986
Enamel on tarp with silk banner,
    125½ x 186½ (318.8 x 473.7)
Collection of the artist

THE STARN TWINS

Untitled, 1987
Installation of toned silver print
  photographs, various sizes, including
  Christ (Stretched), 1985–86; *Double Stark
  Portrait in Swirl*, 1985–86; and *Mark
  Morrisroe*, 1985–86
Stux Gallery, New York and Boston

DONALD SULTAN

Detroit Oct 31 1986, 1986
Latex and tar on tile over board, 96 x 96
  (243.8 x 243.8)
Blum Helman Gallery, New York

*Three Apples Three Pears and a
  Lemon Dec 6 1986*, 1986
Oil, spackle, and tar on tile over board,
  97 x 97 (246.4 x 246.4)
Blum Helman Gallery, New York

Veracruz Nov 18 1986, 1986
Latex and tar on tile over board,
  96½ x 96½ (245.1 x 245.1)
Collection of Laura Carpenter

PHILIP TAAFFE

Quad Cinema, 1986
Acrylic, enamel, and linoprint collage on
  canvas, 88 x 89 (223.5 x 226.1)
Galerie Paul Maenz, Cologne

Nativity (Red, White), 1986
Acrylic and silkscreen collage on canvas,
  65 x 90 (165.1 x 228.6)
Collection of Frederick Roos

Yellow, Grey, 1986
Acrylic and silkscreen collage on canvas,
  84 x 55¼ (213.4 x 140.3)
Collection of Paul Maenz

RICHARD TUTTLE

Orange Blue Yellow, 1986
Mixed media, 16 x 16 x 12
  (40.6 x 40.6 x 30.5)
Blum Helman Gallery, New York

Silver Mercury, 1986
Mixed media, 16 x 10 x 8
  (40.6 x 25.4 x 20.3)
Blum Helman Gallery, New York

Yellow "V" Against Brown, 1986
Mixed media, 16 x 12 x 4
  (40.6 x 30.5 x 10.2)
Blum Helman Gallery, New York

BRUCE WEBER

Studio Wall, 1987
Installation of toned silver print
  photographs, various sizes, including
  Chris Isaak in Limo, New York City, 1985;
  *Karch "Special K" Kiraly, U.S. Olympic
  Volleyball Player, New York City*, 1985;
  David at 29 Palms Inn, Joshua Tree, 1986
Robert Miller Gallery, New York

GRAHAME WEINBREN
AND ROBERTA FRIEDMAN

The Erl King, 1986
Video installation: video disks, micro-
  computer, touch-sensitive monitor,
  and monitor
Collection of the artists

TERRY WINTERS

Dumb Compass, 1985
Oil on linen, 94½ x 132½ (240 x 336.6)
The Saatchi Collection, London

Pitch Lake, 1985
Oil on linen, 90 x 121 (228.6 x 307.3)
Collection of Eli and Edythe L. Broad

Asphaltum, 1986
Oil on linen, 88 x 120 (223.5 x 304.8)
Collection of Eli and Edythe L. Broad

FILM AND VIDEO

ERICKA BECKMAN

Cinderella, 1986
16mm film, color, sound; 24 minutes
Lent by the artist
Film Program II

JAMES BENNING

Landscape Suicide, 1986
16mm film, color, sound; 95 minutes
Lent by the artist; distributed by the
    Film-makers' Cooperative, New York
Film Program III

ALAN BERLINER

The Family Album, 1986
16mm, black and white, sound; 60 minutes
Lent by the artist
Film Program VI

STEPHANIE BEROES

The Dream Screen, 1986
16mm film, black and white, sound;
    45 minutes
Lent by the artist
Film Program VII

PEER BODE

Blind Fields, 1985
Videotape, color, sound; 5 minutes

Animal Migrations, 1985
Videotape, color and black and white,
    sound; 11 minutes

Lent by the artist
Video Program VII

JOAN BRADERMAN

Joan Does Dynasty, 1986
Videotape, color, sound; 31 minutes
Lent by the artist; distributed by Video
    Data Bank, Chicago, and Paper Tiger
    Television, New York
Video Program VI

HANS BREDER

My TV Dictionary: The Drill, 1986
Videotape, color, sound; 3 minutes

My TV Dictionary: The Helicopter,
    1986
Videotape, color, sound; 3 minutes

Lent by the artist
Video Program VII

JUAN DOWNEY

J.S. Bach, 1986
Videotape, color, sound; 28 minutes
Lent by the artist; distributed by Electronic
    Arts Intermix, New York
Video Program II

STEVE FAGIN

*The Amazing Voyage of Gustave
    Flaubert and Raymond Roussel*, 1986
Videotape, color, sound; 74 minutes
Lent by the artist; distributed by
    The Kitchen, New York, and
    Video Data Bank, Chicago
Video Program I

ERNIE GEHR

Signal—Germany on the Air, 1985
16mm film, color, sound; 38 minutes
Lent by the artist; distributed by the
    Film-makers' Cooperative, New York,
    and Canyon Cinema, San Francisco
Film Program VIII

PAUL GLABICKI

Object Conversation, 1985
16mm film, color, sound; 10 minutes
Lent by the artist; distributed by Canyon
    Cinema, San Francisco, and Picture
    Start, Champaign, Illinois
Film Program VI

SHALOM GOREWITZ

Run, 1986
Videotape, color, sound; 3 minutes
Lent by the artist; distributed by
    Electronic Arts Intermix, New York
Video Program VII

DAN GRAHAM

Rock My Religion, 1986
Videotape, color, sound; 57 minutes
Lent by the artist; distributed by
    Electronic Arts Intermix, New York
Video Program III

BARBARA HAMMER

Optic Nerve, 1985
16mm film, color, sound; 16 minutes
Lent by the artist; distributed by the
    Film-makers' Cooperative, Parabola,
    New York, and Canyon Cinema,
    San Francisco
Film Program VII

GARY HILL

URA ARU (the backside exists),
    1985–86
Videotape, color, sound; 28 minutes
Lent by the artist; distributed by
    Electronic Arts Intermix, New York
Video Program VII

LEANDRO KATZ

The Visit, 1986
16mm film, black and white, sound;
    30 minutes
Lent by the artist
Film Program II

ERNEST MARRERO AND
    SUSAN KOUGUELL

Before the Rise of Premonition, 1985
16mm film, color, sound; 20 minutes
Lent by the artists; distributed by the
    Film-makers' Cooperative, New York
Film Program II

NINA MENKES

*Magdalena Viraga: The Story of a
    Red Sea Crossing*, 1986
16mm film, color, sound; 90 minutes
Produced with Tinka Menkes and
    Claire Aguilar
Lent by the artist
Film Program V

SHERRY MILLNER

Scenes from the Micro War, 1986
Videotape, color, sound; 24 minutes
Lent by the artist; distributed by Women
    Make Movies, New York
Video Program V

YVONNE RAINER

The Man Who Envied Women, 1985
16mm film, color, sound; 130 minutes
Lent by the artist; distributed by First Run
    Features, New York
Film Program I

RACHEL REICHMAN

The Riverbed, 1986
16mm film, black and white, sound;
    95 minutes
Lent by the artist
Film Program IV

MARTHA ROSLER

*If It's Too Bad to Be True, It Could Be
    DISINFORMATION*, 1985
Videotape, color, sound; 17 minutes
Lent by the artist; distributed by
    Video Data Bank, Chicago
Video Program V

MATTHEW SCHLANGER

Lumpy Banger, 1986
Videotape, color, sound; 1 minute
Before the Flood, 1985
Videotape, color, sound; 4 minutes

Lent by the artist
Video Program VII

WARREN SONBERT

The Cup and the Lip, 1986
16mm film, color, silent; 20 minutes
Lent by the artist; distributed by the
    Film-makers' Cooperative, New York,
    and Canyon Cinema, San Francisco
Film Program VIII

SKIP SWEENEY

My Mother Married Wilbur Stump,
    1985
Videotape, color and black and white,
    sound; 28 minutes
Lent by the artist; distributed by The
    Kitchen, Electronic Arts Intermix,
    New York, and Video Free America,
    San Francisco
Video Program VI

TRINH T. MINH-HA

Naked Spaces: Living Is Round, 1985
16mm film, color, sound; 134 minutes
Lent by the artist; distributed by Women
    Make Movies, The Museum of Modern
    Art, and Third World Newsreel,
    New York
Film Program IX

BILL VIOLA

I Do Not Know What It Is I Am Like,
    1986
Videotape, color, sound; 89 minutes
Lent by the artist; distributed by Electronic
    Arts Intermix, New York
Video Program IV

BRUCE AND NORMAN
    YONEMOTO

Kappa, 1986
Videotape, color, sound; 26 minutes
Produced in collaboration with Mike Kelley
Lent by the artists; distributed by Video
    Data Bank, Chicago, and Electronic
    Arts Intermix, New York
Video Program II

FILM AND VIDEO SCHEDULE
Second-floor Film and Video Gallery

Film

PROGRAM I
Yvonne Rainer
March 31–April 4; May 22–26

PROGRAM II
Ernest Marrero and Susan Kouguell
Leandro Katz
Ericka Beckman
April 5–10; May 27–30

PROGRAM III
James Benning
April 11–16; May 31–June 4

PROGRAM IV
Rachel Reichman
April 17–22; June 5–9

PROGRAM V
Nina Menkes
April 23–28; June 10–13

PROGRAM VI
Alan Berliner
Paul Glabicki
April 29–May 3; June 14–18

PROGRAM VII
Stephanie Beroes
Barbara Hammer
May 5–9; June 19–23

PROGRAM VIII
Ernie Gehr
Warren Sonbert
May 10–15; June 24–27

PROGRAM IX
Trinh T. Minh-ha
May 16–21; June 28–July 2

Video

PROGRAM I
Steve Fagin
March 31–April 4; April 29–May 3;
May 22–26; June 14–18

PROGRAM II
Bruce and Norman Yonemoto
Juan Downey
April 5–10; May 27–30

PROGRAM III
Dan Graham
April 11–16; May 31–June 4

PROGRAM IV
Bill Viola
April 17–22; May 16–21;
June 5–9; June 28–July 2

PROGRAM V
Martha Rosler
Sherry Millner
April 23–28; June 10–13

PROGRAM VI
Skip Sweeney
Joan Braderman
May 5–9; June 19–23

PROGRAM VII
Gary Hill
Peer Bode
Matthew Schlanger
Shalom Gorewitz
Hans Breder
May 10–15; June 24–27